How to get TOP GRADES in your exams

D1092929

HOW TO GET TOP GRADES IN YOUR EXAMS

First published in 2015 as *A* in Exams*
This revised and updated edition © Summersdale Publishers Ltd, 2017

Images © Shutterstock

Summersdale Publishers Ltd
46 West Street
Chichester
West Sussex
PO19 1RP
UK

www.summersdale.com

Printed and bound in Croatia

ISBN: 978-1-78685-004-1

Substantial discounts on bulk quantities of Summersdale books are available to corporations, professional associations and other organisations. For details contact general enquiries: telephone: +44 (0) 1243 771107, fax: +44 (0) 1243 786300 or email: enquiries@summersdale.com.

How to get

TOP

GRADES

in your exams

TIPS + ADVICE FOR ACHIEVING SUCCESS

Ross Dickinson

ABOUT THE AUTHOR

Ross Dickinson has taught English at Key Stage 3, 4 and 5 in a number of schools across the UK. He currently lives in Cornwall and has worked with *LendMeYourLiteracy*, an organisation which nurtures and celebrates children's writing.

CONTENTS

INTRODUCTION:

So here it is.

For your whole life (or your whole life so far), your teachers have been telling you pretty much one thing and one thing only... your exams matter.

Perhaps, to help intensify that statement, they've even added a few keywords here and there: 'career', 'UCAS', 'university', 'prospects', 'your adult life'. Sound familiar? The fact is, your teachers are absolutely right. The exams you are about to take absolutely do matter. But what your teachers sometimes forget is that when they pile all that pressure on you, it can only lead to one thing: stress.

But the truth is that stress doesn't actually need to be a part of exams. Sure, exams need to be revised for, prepared for and planned for, but that doesn't mean that you need to get stressed. With the right amount of all those things just mentioned – revision, preparation, planning – plus a healthy dose of good strategies that you can use both in and out of the classroom, you can approach your exams with just the right mindset it takes to pass and to succeed.

And it is exactly those good and healthy strategies that this book is packed with – strategies that put you on the right path to face your exams and give you all you need to pass them with flying colours.

So – do you want those crucial top grades? And do you want to achieve them with the least amount of stress possible? Then read on. This book will tell you how to do both.

How to use this book

How to Get Top Grades in Your Exams isn't just any old revision guide. Instead, this is a revision guidebook, and like all guidebooks it can be followed step by step in a chronological fashion. It will take you through the entire revision process, from the moment your exams first appear on the horizon to the moment you sit them, and through all the moments in between, so that you know exactly what you need to be doing and exactly in what order.

At the end of each chapter, we've provided a checklist of all the things you will have learnt. Make sure you've done these things before turning to the next chapter, and physically show that you've done them by ticking them off, making a note of them or even sharing them with your friends. This will help to consolidate the learning in your mind, proving that you are ready to continue.

ALONG THE WAY, *you will also encounter real-life exam tips and stories. We know that each student is different, so we've collected these helpful tips and stories from a wide range of people. This way, we know that every one of you reading this book will find something that you can relate to, and which will help you with your own revision.*

The most important thing of all

We're going to start this book with perhaps the most important thing of all – and that is YOU.

Never forget that the exams you are about to take are YOUR exams. They are not there to make your teachers feel that they've done their jobs properly. They are not there to test your mum and dad's parenting skills. They are not there to mark out your school's position in the league table. They are for YOU and YOU ALONE.

Now, this might sound a little scary at first. It might put a whole lot of responsibility on you that you don't necessarily feel you can handle at this stage in your life. But it's really not that scary at all – especially not when we add to it the second most important thing to remember:

THE EXAMS ARE NOT DESIGNED TO TRIP YOU UP.

Exams are not your enemy

All of your exams will ask you about things that you have learnt, things that you do know. They are not there to catch you out or make you look stupid. They are there simply to assess your knowledge on the subjects you have been studying, and then to reward you for your answers.

REMEMBER: *Exams give marks for the things you get right. They never deduct marks for the things you get wrong.*

So let's put those two points together. Exams are there to help YOU show the world what you can do, and not what you can't do. And, believe me, you can do and you know probably far more than you're even aware of. Think about it. If you're 14 then you've been at school for nine years! If you're 18 then you've been at school for 13 years!

Sure, you've been doing plenty of other stuff in that time – you've been growing up, you've been making friends you'll have for the rest of your life, you've been discovering the hobbies you enjoy and the things that you like to do and might like to do more of in the future – but over all those years the thing you've been doing more of than anything else is learning.

REAL-LIFE EXAM TIPS

Some exams allow you to take books in with you, and some of these allow you to make notes in the books. If you have one of these exams, fill your book with as much information as you can to prompt you when you get into the exam hall.

MARCIE

You are amazing – no really, you are! You are a learner, and you're a pretty incredible one, at that. Think about a job that a member of your family does. Maybe they've been doing that job for nine years, maybe even for 13. They've been learning, too – all that time they've been doing the job, they've been learning how to do it as well as they possibly can. But – whether their job is being a mechanic or a doctor or a computer programmer or a teacher – the fact is that they've only been learning one thing. And you? You've been learning ten, 12, maybe even 15 different things all at the same time!

When was the last time your mum read a Shakespeare play, differentiated equations and conducted a survey on eating habits – all in the same day? When was the last time your dad wrote a persuasive letter, practised his French and read about World War Two – all in the same day? When was the last time your uncle created a PowerPoint presentation, conducted an experiment on heat convection and played a game of tennis – all in the same day? Not for a long, long time, I can tell you.

Whereas you – well, you do all of that each and every day, and you have been doing it each and every day for years and years now. You are an absolute wealth of knowledge, a fountain of intelligence, and you hold the answers to so much that adults can only guess at.

So be confident

Exams are there to help you show off that knowledge, that intelligence, those answers. The people who write exam papers (and this may be difficult to believe but, trust me, it's true) want you to show the world what a brilliant learner you are. Because you are, and there's no denying it. YOU are.

So – the first two steps to your exams are simple ones: understand that they are for you alone and that they are there to help you succeed. Now you know that, we can get on to the more specific stuff – making sure you get those top grades.

CHECKLIST

This first checklist is perhaps the easiest of all of them, but it is no less important. To get yourself in the right frame of mind and to ensure that you will end up getting the grades you deserve, it is absolutely crucial that you understand and take to heart the following two sentences:

❑ *I understand that my exams are there for me and no one else.*

❑ *I understand that my exams are designed to help me succeed at what I do best.*

REAL-LIFE EXAM STORIES: TANYA

I was painfully shy when I was a teenager. If you weren't one of my closest friends, then I simply wouldn't talk to you. It wasn't that I didn't want to. I just couldn't.

My shyness didn't affect my life too much – well, not until my GCSEs. I remember that Year 10 was fine, and so was the first term of Year 11. I was keeping up with everything and getting good grades. My teachers and my parents seemed pleased with my progress, and I was too.

But then, just after the February half-term break, it all started to get too much for me. It wasn't that I didn't understand anything I was revising – my problem was that I didn't know exactly *what* I should be revising. There was so much! The moment I began to focus on one subject, I'd just see this huge mass of information, and I had no idea which bits I should be retaining and which bits I should ignore. It became overwhelming and because I was so shy, rather than asking for help as I should have done, I didn't tell anyone, and the feeling just got worse and worse until I pretty much shut down. I stopped listening in class. I stopped doing my homework. I failed every single one of my mock exams.

A meeting was organised for me, my form tutor and my parents. They kept asking me again and again what was wrong, and I desperately wanted to tell them, but I was too shy. It was like the words were there in my brain, but they got lost somewhere on the way to my mouth.

It was my best friend Kirsty who saved me. She knew me better than anyone and, when she found me crying in the toilets not long before study leave, she marched me straight to our Maths teacher and said: 'Sir, Tanya needs help with her revision, but she's too shy to ask.' The teacher immediately told me to come back at lunchtime, where he would sit down with me and go through anything I wanted, one-on-one. Kirsty then took me to each of my teachers in turn, and every single one of them did the same thing – they all offered their own one-on-one help.

Sitting there with each teacher – just me and him or her – wasn't easy, especially when I had to explain why I was struggling. But the moment I did, I felt better. Each teacher talked me through my worries, and told me exactly what I should be revising and what I didn't need to. Sometimes all I needed was ten minutes with a teacher, and sometimes I had a weekly after-school session. I was able to manage my revision, and I stopped feeling so overwhelmed.

I passed each of my GCSEs, maybe not quite as well as I had been hoping, but at least I passed. I'm so grateful to my teachers for helping me, and I only wish that I had gone to them sooner. Looking back on it all now, I don't know why I was so shy. I guess I thought they would be angry with me or tell me off or something. But not one of them did. All they wanted was to help me. And they really did.

REAL-LIFE EXAM TIPS

I did most of my revision alone, but once a week I got together with my friends. We'd discuss what we'd revised, we'd test each other and we'd help each other with things we might each be struggling with. I loved these meetings; I learned loads from them – mostly that I wasn't alone!

RUTH

CHAPTER 2: WHAT KIND OF LEARNER ARE YOU?

Now that we've established that your exams are about you and you alone, the next thing you need to decide is – what kind of learner are you?

Have you ever wondered why, say, you're really good at English but not so good at Maths; or why your friend always gets selected for the A teams in PE but struggles to concentrate in History; or why your other friend seems to have a real knack for modern foreign languages but just can't get his head around most IT lessons?

Maybe it's not even about different subjects, but different areas within one subject. Maybe you can solve every equation your Maths teacher sets you, but when it comes to geometry you're stumped at the first step? Maybe you read a book a week and write reviews on them, which always get you top marks, but when you need to give a speech to the rest of the class you're a gibbering wreck who stumbles through the words and can't even make eye contact with your best friend?

If this all sounds familiar, it's because it should. Everybody knows somebody who seems to do well at everything (and if you don't know someone like that, then it's probably you), but, for most of us, we tend to excel in some subjects and not do so well in others. There are some subjects that we just love and others we could do without.

This is not a bad thing. In fact, it's the way of the world. It's the way society works. Some of us need to be good at some things; others need to be good at other things. If we could all do everything equally, then we'd never progress as a species. No one person can be brilliant at everything, but every single person – you included – is brilliant at something.

This is what we call 'multiple intelligences'. There is no such thing as someone who is not intelligent. Everyone is intelligent, but in their own different way. So if you find it difficult to write an essay for 45 minutes straight but rule supreme on the football pitch, it doesn't mean you're stupid – it just means your intelligence lies in your ability to perfectly co-ordinate your mind with your body. If you can understand the language patterns of French or German or Spanish with ease but find long division difficult – again, that doesn't mean you're stupid, it just means that your intelligence lies in language acquisition rather than mathematical reasoning. If you know the inner workings of an engine like the back of your hand but can't grasp the intervals of a musical scale – well, you know where I'm going with this.

As I said before, WE ARE ALL INTELLIGENT, but we are all intelligent in our different ways. And, let's be honest, if we were all the same, then it would make for a very dull world.

REAL-LIFE EXAM TIPS

I make up silly stories which include the details of the things I need to remember. So my story to remember the names of Henry VIII's wives starts with Catherine driving down to Aragon to take Anne bowling...

DYLAN

This doesn't mean, however, that you can only achieve top grades in the subjects that you find yourself the most intelligent in; quite the contrary. In fact, when we understand where our own intelligence lies, we can then use that to do our best in all areas.

First, however, you need to decide what kind of learner you are. Knowing this – knowing exactly where your intelligence lies – will help you with your revision strategies for your exams.

There are three main kinds of learner:

01 VISUAL – learns mostly through seeing.
02 AUDITORY – learns mostly through hearing.
03 KINAESTHETIC – learns mostly through doing.

Want to know what kind of learner you are? Simply take the test in the next chapter.

REAL-LIFE EXAM TIPS

I always find it useful to use different colours for my notes. Choosing how to use the colours helps me organise my thoughts before I even start writing.

MIKE

How to get TOP GRADES in your exams

CHECKLIST

☐ *I know that there are different kinds of learner.*

☐ *I know that if I am struggling in one or two subjects, this does not mean I am stupid.*

☐ *I know which subjects I am strong in. (HINT: Perhaps note these subjects down at the bottom of this page.)*

....
....
....
....
....
....
....
....
....
....
....
....
....

CHAPTER 3: VISUAL, AUDITORY OR KINAESTHETIC?

Q1 – When not studying, you like to unwind by:
a   Playing a sport or game
b   Listening to music
c   Reading a book

Q2 – You are given a brand new computer with an operating system you haven't used before. Do you:
a   Just start using it and work it out as you go along?
b   Get someone to tell you how to use it?
c   Read the instructions?

Q3 – When you get distracted in class, do you find that you:
a   Fiddle with things?
b   Sing or hum a tune to yourself?
c   Doodle?

Q4 – The lessons you find easiest are the ones where you:

a   Learn by doing the thing itself

b   Get verbal instructions

c   Read about what you have to do

Q5 – When someone has done something nice for you, do you first:

a   Hug them?

b   Tell them thank you?

c   Smile?

Q6 – A story is best when:

a   You can act it out

b   It is read to you

c   You read it yourself

Q7 – Which of these kinds of celebrities would you rather be?

a   Olympic medallist

b   Singer

c   Movie star

Q8 – Think of your best friend. What do you think of first?

a   How they make you feel

b   The things they've said to you

c   What they look like

Q9 – Which of these puzzles would you prefer to do?

a   A Rubik's cube

b   Name That Tune

c   Spot the Difference

Q10 – You remember directions best when:

a   You have been taken along the route before

b   Someone tells you the directions

c   You have a map to follow

Your answers

If you answered mostly As then you are a KINAESTHETIC learner.

If you answered mostly Bs then you are an AUDITORY learner.

If you answered mostly Cs then you are a VISUAL learner.

KINAESTHETIC

Kinaesthetic learners learn best when they get to take part in something – they prefer subjects such as PE, Drama or Design Technology. They do best in lessons that involve practicals and physical learning.

AUDITORY

Auditory learners learn best when they use their sense of hearing – they prefer subjects such as Music and modern foreign languages. They do best in lessons that involve lots of talking and verbal interaction.

VISUAL

Visual learners learn best when they use their sense of sight – they prefer subjects such as English, Geography and Maths. They do best in lessons that involve more reading and writing.

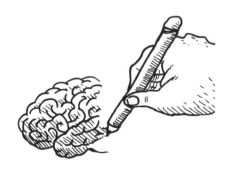

REAL-LIFE EXAM TIPS

The thing that used to help me was condensing my notes down until I had one piece of paper/revision card that just included factual things that I needed to remember, for example, a particular formula/date/definition that I obviously had to know. I took that everywhere with me and would just keep repeating them over and over, making up little rhymes or sayings to help me remember.

AMY

Of course, not everyone falls into just one box. We all tend to lean towards one of the three learning styles more than the other two, but combinations of them do exist. You might find that you're a mostly kinaesthetic learner, but that you do have some visual elements. Or you might find that you are a combination of a visual and an auditory learner.

In the next chapter, you'll find revision tips that are suitable for each kind of learner, but don't be afraid to try out a combination of them. All of these tips are good ways of revising – so there is nothing wrong with experimenting with each bullet point and finding out for yourself which ones help you to revise the most effectively. Do what suits YOU best.

CHECKLIST

❑ *I now know what kind of learner I am.*

I am a... (tick the relevant box):

❑ *Visual learner.*

❑ *Auditory learner.*

❑ *Kinaesthetic learner.*

❑ *Combination of _____ and _____ .*

CHAPTER 4: MAKING THE MOST OF YOUR LEARNING STYLE

So – now that you know what kind of learner you are, how can you use this to make the most of your revision?

KINAESTHETIC

⇨ Give yourself a large space to revise in – maybe even outside!

⇨ Use that space – walk up and down while you're trying to commit something to your memory, or even go out for a walk or ride your bike.

⇨ Act things out. If you're revising a novel or a play, get into the heads of the characters by reading their lines aloud and performing them to an imaginary audience.

⇨ Take regular breaks and do a little bit of exercise during them (nothing too taxing, though!).

⇨ Try to associate things you need to remember with physical actions – i.e. for The Periodic Table, you might <u>C</u>lap <u>O</u>nce for Co (cobalt), or <u>Y</u>awn for Y (yttrium), or <u>S</u>cratch <u>N</u>eck for Sn (tin).

REAL-LIFE EXAM TIPS

My method to learn French verbs was pretty intense, but I got top marks using this method, and so did my little brother. I used to sit in the bath with all the verbs written on posters around the room. I would sit in that bath until I had learned them all. My other thing was to lock myself out of the house and march up and down the garden whilst reciting the important dates of various bits of history.

AGNES

AUDITORY

⇨ Listen to music while you're revising.

⇨ Record yourself reading aloud the notes you made in class, then listen back to the recording.

⇨ Organise revision sessions with friends where you can talk through the subject.

⇨ If you're feeling really brave, try singing your notes!

⇨ Finish your revision session by explaining to your parents what you've just learnt.

VISUAL

⇨ Find a quiet and private space to revise in.

⇨ Read as much as you can – and then draw diagrams and flow charts to illustrate the points you are learning.

⇨ Copy out notes, keywords and phrases onto flash cards and reread them.

⇨ Practise writing under timed conditions.

⇨ Use highlighters to mark out important sections of your notes.

REAL-LIFE EXAM TIPS

For Science and Maths, I liked to write out formulas on file cards. I'd then test myself by pulling out a card at random, looking at the top, and trying to recreate the formula from memory.

JAMES

REAL-LIFE EXAM TIPS

My friends and I got into a really bad habit last year. Whenever we met up on the morning of an exam, we'd talk about how unprepared we felt and we'd just wind ourselves up into a complete panic. So this year we've decided to avoid each other until after the exam, and now I'm going into each one feeling so much calmer.

FRANCIS

CHECKLIST

❑ *I have experimented with each of the revision tips.*

❑ *I have identified the ones that work best for me.*

❑ *I have underlined the tips that work best for me.*

CHAPTER 5: WHERE TO START WITH YOUR REVISION

Knowing where to start with revision can often be the hardest decision a student has to make.

Perhaps you are doing four A levels and are about to take your exams. Perhaps you are doing 14 GCSEs and are about to take your exams. Perhaps each of those subjects doesn't just have one exam, either. Perhaps there are two, three, four or even more for separate modules.

When you're faced with a month of impending and relentless exams that seem like they'll never end, it can be incredibly daunting.

How on earth can you possibly revise it all?

If you've recently found yourself asking this question, then don't worry – you're not alone. Thousands of people your age are asking exactly the same question right now; and hundreds of thousands of people your age have asked exactly the same question each year for decades.

The fact is, it is very difficult to set down one perfect revision strategy that will suit every single student. As we've seen, we all learn in different ways and we all need to take advantage of those different ways in order to revise best.

But that's not something you need to worry about anymore. In fact, you're already far ahead of the rest because you've got this book. This book will help you to design a revision plan that will perfectly suit your individual needs.

REAL-LIFE EXAM TIPS

I used to write out my revision rather than trying to learn it in my head as the physical act of writing seemed to lock things in better.

DAVID

Step one – Find your exam timetable

Get hold of your exam timetable. Your form tutor may have already given this to you, but if not then ask them for it. Schools should give each of their students a personalised timetable which shows them all of the dates and times of their upcoming exams, so don't be afraid to ask.

Step two – Put it where you'll always see it

Once you have your exam timetable, pin it up on the wall directly above where you revise (this might be at a desk in your bedroom, at the dining room table, or even on your bed). If possible, make copies of it and pin it up in different places around your house, or glue a copy into your planner. Very soon, this will be the personal calendar you will live by and it is important that you know it intimately.

Step three – List your exam subjects

Make a list of all the subjects that you have exams in. Some of your subjects may be purely based on coursework, or controlled or practical assessments, so it is important to know which ones you need to revise for and which ones you don't.

It might be the case that you have already completed a subject and taken your GCSE or A level through coursework you have done throughout the year. If you are ever unsure, ask your teacher. Don't be afraid to nag them – remember, they want you to get top grades just as much as you do.

Step four – Work out how important each exam is

All subjects are equal, but all exams might not be. Some weigh more towards your final grade in that subject than others. In the list you made for Step Three, note down next to each exam how long it is and – if you can find out – what percentage of your GCSE or A level it is worth. Don't forget that some subjects may award you more than one qualification (for example, in most cases, English at GCSE level will actually give you two GCSEs – GCSE English and GCSE English Literature). Again, if you're unsure of anything, ask your teacher – and, if you're still unsure, ask them again and again until you know exactly what they mean. Don't forget, these are YOUR exams.

Step five – Make a space for the new list

Pin the list you have just made up on to your wall next to your exam timetable.

Step six – Work out the time you have left

Work out how many days there are until your first exam. While it is possible to continue revising during your exam period, this doesn't mean that you should revise for your exams in the order in which they come. The best approach is to spread your revision out for all subjects equally in the time you have before they begin. This will help you to manage your time more effectively and not get bogged down in day-after-day revision of one single subject. The worst thing to do is leave your revision for your last exam until the very end. Don't forget, exams are exhausting things, and once you've begun them you'll find it difficult to keep up the intensity of your revision.

Mon	Tue	Wed	Thu	Fri	Weekend

Step seven – Create your revision timetable

Once you've worked out how many days there are until your first exam, try to divide that time into separate blocks of revision for each of your subjects. The timings of these blocks will be different for everybody – some students are given 'study leave' while others aren't; some students will have after-school activities or part-time jobs, which they need to work around; some students will only have four subjects to revise for while others will have 14. Whatever your situation, the key thing is that you mark out your free time over the coming months and set yourself a plan of how you will use that time to revise. Having it there in front of you is a very powerful visual tool and will keep you on track so that you don't neglect some subjects in favour of others without realising it. Using your planner or the calendar on your phone or computer can be helpful, but the best way is to create a separate revision timetable which you can fill in and pin up next to your exam timetable, so that you can always keep track of what you need to be revising. Here's a helpful template you can photocopy and fill in to suit your needs best.

REVISION BLOCKS						
Timings:						
Monday						
Tuesday						
Wednesday						
Thursday						
Friday						
Weekend						

Here's an example of how one student filled it in:

REVISION BLOCKS

Timings:	9 a.m.–9.40 a.m.	10 a.m.–10.40 a.m.	11 a.m.–11.40 a.m.	12 noon–12.40 p.m.	2 p.m.–2.40 p.m.	3 p.m.–3.40 p.m.
Monday	English	Drama Studies – Practical Assessment preparation (50 per cent)	Higher Maths – Paper 1 (50 per cent)	English Literature – Paper 2 (50 per cent)	Drama Studies – Written Assessment (50 per cent)	Higher Maths – Paper 2 (50 per cent)
Tuesday	FREE	Higher Maths – Paper 2 (50 per cent)	FREE	Drama Studies – Written Assessment (50 per cent)	FREE	English Literature – Paper 2 (50 per cent)
Wednesday	Higher Maths – Paper 1 (50 per cent)	FREE	FREE	Drama Studies – Practical Assessment preparation (50 per cent)	English Literature – Paper 1 (50 per cent)	FREE
Thursday	FREE	Higher Maths – Paper 1 (50 per cent)	FREE	Drama Studies – Practical Assessment preparation (50 per cent)	FREE	English Literature – Paper 1 (50 per cent)
Friday	English Literature – Paper 1 (50 per cent)	Drama Studies – Practical Assessment preparation (50 per cent)	Higher Maths – Paper 1 (50 per cent)	English Literature – Paper 2 (50 per cent)	Drama Studies – Written Assessment (50 per cent)	Higher Maths – Paper 2 (50 per cent)
Weekend	(Saturday) Drama Studies – Written Assessment (50 per cent)	(Saturday) Higher Maths – Paper 2 (50 per cent)	(Saturday) English Literature – Paper 2 (50 per cent)	FREE	FREE	FREE

REAL-LIFE EXAM TIPS

I sing EVERYTHING. If I can fit something I need to remember to the lyrics of a song I love, then that's it, I'll never forget it.

ELEYNIE

TOP TIPS FOR FILLING IN YOUR REVISION TIMETABLE

⇨ Try to vary the times you revise each subject from day to day.

⇨ Leave time for breaks between each session – you'll need them!

⇨ If you're on study leave, treat your days as if you were still at school. Revise when you should be in lessons. And, if you are still at school, mark off each lesson as revision time – that counts, too!

⇨ Make sure you leave time for a good lunch halfway through the day.

⇨ Allow yourself to have regular snacks.

⇨ Revise in short bursts. Don't spend more than one hour or less than 20 minutes on your revision before taking a break.

⇨ Don't revise right up until bedtime. Whether you're at school or on study leave, when you finish your revision you need some leisure time. See friends, do some exercise, watch some TV, play a game. Everyone needs to unwind after a hard day's work.

Have you followed all of those steps? If not, then put this book down right now and follow them. If you have, however, then read on.

CHECKLIST

❑ *I have my exam timetable.*

❑ *I know which subjects I have exams for.*

❑ *I know how long I have left before each exam.*

❑ *I have created my revision timetable.*

CHAPTER 6: PREPARING YOUR REVISION SPACE

No matter what kind of learner you are – visual, auditory or kinaesthetic – it is hugely important that you create a space for yourself in which you can revise without interruptions. For most students, this is their bedroom – a sanctuary of privacy. However, some of us have to share our bedrooms; and some of us find it difficult to revise in a place designed for sleeping rather than working! Whatever your situation, designate a part of your home as YOUR revision space. Tell your parents and your brothers and sisters that – until your exams are over – this is your office: this is your place of work.

And, if they still don't believe you when you tell them how important it is that you have your own revision space, we've provided an official letter on the next page for you to fill in and show them. It has the Top Grades seal of approval and it never fails.

The Top Grades in Exams Team
c/o Summersdale Publishers Ltd
46 West Street
Chichester
West Sussex
PO19 1RP

Dear _____,

We hereby inform you that _____ has officially designated the _____ area of your home as their revision space. This begins with immediate effect and will last until _____.

Do not be alarmed. This part of your home will fall back to its normal state by the date given above. If you wish to appeal this decision, please direct all requests towards the Top Grades in Exams Team rather than _____, as he/she will be too busy revising to deal with your enquiries.

As an officially designated revision space, it must remain as a quiet and secure area where _____ can revise without impediment. The only interruptions that will be tolerated are those that come in the form of sandwiches.

We thank you for your time,

The Top Grades in Exams Team

REAL-LIFE EXAM TIPS

Whenever I was reading or writing or rewriting my notes, I would sit at my desk in my bedroom. However, when I wanted to commit things to memory, I found it much more effective if I walked as I recited them to myself – either to the shops and back or even just pacing around my room.

CHLOE

TOP TIP: *If you still can't find a good place to revise at home – don't forget, your school is also a resource! Even if you're on study leave, you are still allowed to return to school to revise there. The library is a wonderful place to revise. And don't forget that your school doesn't have the only library in the world. Visit your local public library – not only might it be open for longer and have even more resources than your school, but the staff will love it when you tell them you've just popped in for a spot of quiet revision!*

No matter where your revision space is, you can make the most of it by following these simple dos and don'ts.

Do:

⇨ Do use a good chair, which is comfortable but has a straight back. You will probably have to spend a lot of time sitting down while revising (and even more time sitting down when the exams come along), so don't give yourself an injury through bad posture.

⇨ Do drink plenty of water while revising. The best way is to have a bottle beside you, which you top up every time you leave your revision space.

⇨ Because of the above, do make sure your revision space is close to a toilet.

⇨ If you feel yourself losing concentration, do take a quick break – even just for two minutes. Do some stretches; flex the muscles in your fingers; rotate your wrists; do a really big fake yawn. Try it now! It will oxygenate your blood and you'll find yourself much more focused afterwards.

⇨ Do turn your phone off.

⇨ Do surround yourself with the books you need – both your textbooks and class books. Try to have them within your reach.

How to get TOP GRADES in your exams

⇨ Do ask for help whenever you need it. Your teachers and parents will be able to help you, but so too might your brother and/or sister – you never know, so don't be afraid to ask!

⇨ Do experiment with different approaches. If you've read the same passage over and over again and it's just not going in, then try reading it aloud, copying it out, highlighting sections, or even singing it!

⇨ Do keep a small notebook at hand for those unexpected flashes of inspiration. If you're rereading *Lord of the Flies* and suddenly get an idea for your final Art project while queuing for lunch in the school cafeteria or riding the bus home, note it down before you forget it.

Don't:

⇨ Don't spend all your time at a computer. Try to vary the types of revision you do – change to writing with a pen or reading from a book – so that you're not always staring at a computer screen.

⇨ Don't revise for over an hour without taking a break – even a quick one.

⇨ Don't allow yourself to get seduced by the Internet (we'll talk more about the Internet in Chapter 12). Social networking sites in particular can be incredibly distracting. Of course, you will need to use the Internet for research purposes, but try to limit it to that. One good trick is to create a list of favourites of the websites you use for research and then refer to this and this only whenever you go online.

⇨ Don't leave a subject if you get stuck on it. You should keep going until you find the answers you need. You are more likely to return to a piece of work if you have left it at a place you understand. (I should probably add here that, if you really do feel like you've hit a brick wall, make a note of your difficulty and then talk to your teacher about it as soon as you possibly can.)

⇨ Don't overeat at lunch. It is extremely important that you keep yourself well fed while revising, but eating too much will send all your blood to your stomach to digest, leaving none left for your brain to revise. (While we're on the subject, try not to eat in your revision space. Keep your revision time and your meals as separate entities. This will help to train you so that you don't get a distracting attack of the munchies during your actual exams – when eating is most definitely not an option!)

⇨ Don't leave all your revision until the last minute. You can use the handy tips in Chapter 10 to help you avoid this. Don't overwork yourself (people who leave their revision until the last minute tend to overwork themselves). Make sure you give yourself plenty of breaks, and set a time for the end of each day when you will finish.

⇨ Don't just stick to the core texts. You should read around your subjects as much as possible to gain extra insights which will ensure you those valuable top grades. (But don't let this put you off your core texts. They are called core texts for a reason. They should form the basis of everything else you revise).

CHECKLIST

❑ *I have designated my revision space.*

❑ *I have followed the dos and don'ts to ensure I work best in my revision space.*

REAL-LIFE EXAM STORIES: KAROLINA

I know this is going to sound like a complete humblebrag, but being smart can sometimes hold you back.

Let me just flesh that out a little. When I was at school, I was considered one of the smart ones (the most common word teachers used to describe me was 'bright'). I was in all the top sets. I got good grades in most subjects without really trying. Everyone was confident in me and I was confident in myself.

I know, none of this sounds like it would hold a person back at all, does it? But here's the problem. Because I hardly ever needed to try, I stopped trying altogether. Because everyone was so confident in me, nobody paid me much attention and a lot of the time I was just left to do my own thing. Because I always got good grades anyway, I became complacent. My confidence turned into arrogance.

School had always been a breeze for me, and Year 11 turned out to be just the same. We had loads of practice exams that year, and I seemed to be a bit of a natural at them – I always finished early and got a good mark. I never revised for any of them, and so when the real GCSEs came along I decided I didn't need to revise for them either. I was bright, you see. I was smart. And I would get along just fine without bothering to revise.

I remember finding each exam a lot harder than I had anticipated. I think that all my earlier practice exams had been easier because I had been learning in school each day, so I had it all in my head, whereas during my Study Leave all I did was watch TV all day. However, when it came to my real

GCSEs there was nothing in them that I couldn't answer and I still felt confident that I would do well.

No doubt you know exactly where this is all leading. I'm sure I don't even need to tell you about the day I walked into school to receive my results, and about the shock and horror I felt when I opened that envelope and saw my grades for the first time. I left before any of the teachers could talk to me, and then I took about three hours to walk the ten-minute journey home.

Actually, my grades hadn't been completely awful. I had passed about half of my subjects (albeit barely). But the two I had completely failed were perhaps the two most important: English and Maths.

The following year, I started college. They had almost rejected me based on my grades, but (after lots of discussion) they agreed to accept me so long as I re-took my English and Maths GCSEs. And so, for the next year, while I studied four A-Levels, I also re-studied two GCSEs in special end-of-the-day classes which the college put on for students who, like me, had failed their earlier exams. I no longer felt 'bright'.

The humiliation of it was almost unbearable. I lied to my friends about the classes, pretending I was learning the guitar. My parents were supportive, but I could still see how disappointed they were. At least the classes were small, so the teachers were able to give me much more attention than I was used to. Nevertheless, I hated being there, and so I decided to start trying. I put in extra hours, I did more work than the teachers asked for, I studied independently and I revised endlessly. I would not, I resolved, have to re-take anything ever again.

Again, you probably already know exactly where this is leading. I passed my English and Maths GCSEs. I passed them with flying colours. And, ever since then, I've never stopped trying, and I've achieved a lot to be proud of. But I still can't help but wish that I'd learned to try so much earlier, that I hadn't let my arrogance get the better of me and that I'd revised during Year 11 like all my friends did. That way, I would have avoided all that shock, horror and humiliation, as well as a whole year of extra classes.

CHAPTER 7: OVERCOMING REVISION STRESS

Revision can place a huge strain on the mind and the body. There's no denying the fact that in the months leading up to your exams you will probably have to work harder than you have ever worked before. So it's important that you look after yourself – both physically and mentally – because physical and mental strain can only lead to one thing: STRESS.

Keeping stress levels to a minimum is an absolute must – not only will this help enhance your revision time, it will also help you towards gaining those desired grades.

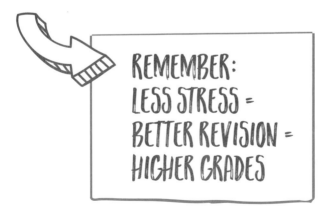

REMEMBER:
LESS STRESS =
BETTER REVISION =
HIGHER GRADES

Nobody knows your body better than you. We all have our limits of endurance and we all understand them intimately. Listen to your body if it's telling you that it's feeling depleted or weak or tired. Sometimes, when our own warning signs pop up, they can be resolved by something as simple as drinking some water, eating more fruit and vegetables, or getting a good night's sleep.

But, when you place yourself under the intense pressures of revision, it can be easy to ignore these warning signs and easy to forget to do those simple things that make for a better you. In fact, sometimes (particularly when you have so much else on your mind) you might not even notice when stress is building up in your body, so you should always build in some time at the end of the day when you can relax.

True exam success does not depend on how you're feeling on the day; it depends on how you allow yourself to feel while you're revising. On the previous page, we included a very simple equation – but it's one that is so important we're going to repeat it:

LESS STRESS =
BETTER REVISION =
HIGHER GRADES

There's another way of putting that:

LESS STRESS = MORE SUCCESS

But how can you overcome that stress, which can sometimes feel like it is an inevitable consequence of revision? In truth, there are a number of ways. Below we have listed five tried-and-tested methods of successfully keeping your stress levels to an absolute minimum.

SET YOURSELF SHORT, ACHIEVABLE GOALS

Your revision does not all need to be done at once. You do not need to know everything there is to know about Chemistry by Friday. Instead, decide at the start of each day what it is you want to achieve, and keep those goals manageable. For example:

⇨   I will write out all my notes of Act 1 Scene 5 of *Romeo and Juliet* by lunchtime.

⇨   I will learn 20 new Spanish nouns in the next half hour.

I will be able to recite all the bone groups by the end of the day.

By keeping your goals short and manageable, you will be able to gradually build up your knowledge as you get closer to your exams. This building up of knowledge is exactly how to get the grades you're after. Remember: cramming everything at once never works.

REAL-LIFE EXAM TIPS

When I first started preparing for my exams, I began to think about all of them at once, and the thought of all those different subjects and papers overwhelmed me. So, after that, each day I would only think about one subject or even just one exam, and wouldn't allow myself to think of any of the others. This helped break it all down into more manageable chunks for me, and I could revise without verging on an anxiety attack!

FRANCESCA

REWARD YOURSELF

When you've achieved each goal, give yourself a treat. This is a process called 'positive reinforcement'. By allowing yourself something pleasurable at the end of a stint of revision, you 'positively reinforce' the good work you have done. Your brain will then start to associate revision with a reward at the end of it. Before you know it, you'll want to revise! Here are some examples of good rewards:

⟹ Free Internet time (allow yourself ten minutes online where you can do anything you want except work).

⟹ A small food or drink treat (a cup of hot chocolate can be blissful at the end of a long day's revision).

⟹ A game (perhaps on your phone you have zombies that need feeding or farms that need tending. Be careful with this one, though – set yourself a strict time limit and stick to it!)

REAL-LIFE EXAM TIPS

Whenever I got too stressed and lonely in
my bedroom during revision sessions, I'd go
downstairs for a biscuit and a chat with my mum.
Her positivity and the sugar from the
biscuit gave me fuel to carry on!

ABBIE

Keep healthy

Stress can often feel like it's all in your head. In fact, if you keep your body healthy it's very likely that your mind will stay healthy, too. We all know the kinds of things we should regularly do to maintain a high level of health – but, when your days are filled with revision, revision, revision, you can often forget the simple things you should do to keep yourself in good working order.

Here are four:

Sleep well

Try to get a good night's sleep every night. Eight hours is optimum, but don't sleep for fewer than six or more than ten. Keep to a regular pattern: go to bed at the same time each night (definitely before midnight) and set your alarm so that you wake up at the same time each morning. Try to resist the urge to nap during the daytime, as this can make it harder to sleep at night.

Eat well

You all know what I'm going to say here, right? It's the usual key phrases: balanced diet, five fruit and veg a day, less sugar, etc. That first phrase, however, is the most important. A balanced diet doesn't have to mean that you should cut out all sugars and fats – in moderation, they can be part of a healthy lifestyle. Sometimes, a bar of chocolate can make for a lovely reward after a particularly gruelling session. Just don't overdo it! (HINT: if you're struggling to satisfy your sweet tooth, frozen grapes are a healthy and delicious alternative to sweets.)

Exercise well

You don't have to go to the gym or run a half marathon every day to exercise well (and, with all your revision, you probably won't have the time!). No matter – simply taking a walk outside, riding your bike for 30 minutes, or even dancing in your bedroom to a few tunes are all excellent ways of exercising.

REAL-LIFE EXAM TIPS

Whenever I needed a break from revision, I'd go for a run. I know that running isn't everyone's cup of tea, but for me it was the perfect way to clear my head after a long revision session and wake myself up for the next one.

JOE

Drink well

Make no mistake, water is your friend. It is so important to stay well hydrated while revising. While there's a chance that caffeine-rich drinks could leave you feeling dehydrated, water will always make you feel better. You should drink plenty of it every day – if not, you run the risk of headaches, grogginess, reduced concentration levels and, of course, stress.

Unsure if you're drinking enough water? Take the pee test!

All right, so this might sound a bit weird, but when you next go for a pee, check out the colour of your urine. If it's deep yellow, then you're not drinking enough. Pee should be very light in colour to show that you're getting enough water.

DON'T CUT YOURSELF OFF *An element of privacy and seclusion can be helpful when revising, but that doesn't mean that you should spend all day every day locked up in your bedroom poring over books. Allow yourself time to properly interact with others – for example, eat your meals with your family rather than taking dinner up to your bedroom so that you can continue revising while you munch.*

And don't forget your friends! They are going through exactly the same thing as you, so organise times when you can meet up, chew the fat and generally blow off some steam together.

STAY POSITIVE! There will be times when you feel like your revision is just too much for one person to handle. These are dark times and they happen to us all, but if you're feeling like that right now, then remember that you are not alone. You should also remember that you can do this. Your teachers entered you for these exams because they knew that you could pass them – if they didn't think you had what it takes, they would have suggested alternatives. More importantly, you are reading this book because you know that you've got what it takes to ace your exams.

So what if you need a little help here and there? Everybody does! Just go back over the four previous strategies, make sure you're sticking to them and stay positive!

CHECKLIST

☐ *I have set myself short, achievable goals.*

☐ *I know how I will reward myself when I achieve each goal.*

☐ *I have decided on the ways in which I will stay healthy.*

☐ *I have worked out times during my revision when I can meet up with others.*

☐ *I will stay positive.*

CHAPTER 8: HOW TO DEAL WITH ANXIETY

So – are you feeling positive? I hope so. You should be. If you have read through and followed all of the advice given in this book so far, you will now be ready to tackle your revision with maximum efficiency. You will be seeing

those brilliant grades on the horizon. You will be visualising success. You will be feeling positive. And, if you are, then feel free to skip this chapter and move on to the next. If, however, you are not, then don't worry – this chapter is for you.

If you are still not feeling ready to begin your revision and still not feeling positive in yourself and your abilities, then it is very likely that you are experiencing anxiety. Anxiety can be a very frightening thing – although it's just an emotion, it can have scary physical side-effects: dizziness, panic attacks, feeling like your heart is beating out of your chest, shortness of breath, heat flushes and fear.

Many students find themselves gripped by anxiety when their exams approach, but it is also something that all humans can be prone to, no matter what age they are. Anxiety affects 25 per cent of people at some point in their lives. So if you're feeling it right now, you're not alone. One in four people have felt or are feeling exactly the same way as you.

If you are affected by anxiety, the first thing you should do is talk to someone about it. This doesn't mean you need to see a psychiatrist – in fact, just telling someone you know and care for about your anxiety (a friend, your parents, a teacher) can make a world of difference. Talking about anxiety is one of the best ways to understand and come to terms with it. In fact, it is highly likely that the person you are speaking to has experienced anxiety themselves and just knowing this can help you to understand that it's a very normal way of feeling. Sometimes, this is all it takes to break down anxiety.

Anxiety is usually caused by a trigger and that trigger is different for everybody. Some people's anxiety can be triggered by an argument, others by money problems, and others by something seemingly inconsequential, such as heavy rain or a crowded bus. A crucial thing to do to help alleviate your anxiety is to work out what has triggered it in the first place. For many people, simply understanding the trigger for their anxiety can help them put a stop to it altogether.

If you are still reading this chapter, it is likely that your anxiety is caused by your impending exams. Fear not, for exam-based anxiety is actually one of the easiest kinds of anxiety to deal with. It all comes down to relaxation. When we experience anxiety, we are not relaxed. In fact, to be relaxed is pretty much the opposite of being anxious. So, when you wake up in the morning ready to face your day of revision or the exam itself and you feel anxious, there are plenty of things you can do which will help you transform your anxiety into relaxation.

REAL-LIFE EXAM TIPS

My biggest problem was that I just couldn't write enough in essay-style exams. The time limit always stressed me out. So I practised writing under timed conditions at home. It didn't even matter what I was writing – sometimes I just made up stories as I went along – but the more I did it the better I got at writing well under timed conditions, and this gave me loads more confidence for my exams.

OLIVIA

Below are three tried-and-tested techniques for overcoming anxiety – and the beauty of them is that they can be done anywhere: on the bus or train, in your bedroom, or even standing outside the exam hall. Why not try them now? We guarantee that each one will help you to feel more relaxed.

Technique one: deep breathing

Anxiety eats into the oxygen in your bloodstream and when your oxygen depletes this can cause you to feel even more anxious, creating a vicious circle of anxiety. One quick and easy way to re-oxygenate your blood is to focus on your breathing.

Inhale deeply through your nose and exhale fully through your mouth. As you breathe in deeply through your nose, think the word 'IN'. As you breathe out fully through your mouth, think the word 'OUT'. Focus your mind just on the two words as you continue to breathe.

This will not only help re-oxygenate your blood, it will also clear your mind of any anxiety.

Technique two: muscle relaxation

Often, anxiety can be the result of tension in the body that we are not even aware of. We might think that we are relaxed when actually all of our muscles are incredibly tense. Conscious muscle relaxation is a brilliant way of easing tension in the body and, with it, easing anxiety in the mind. These simple steps will get you started:

⇨ Tense all the muscles in your feet, hold the tension for three seconds and then relax.

⇨ Tense all the muscles in your legs, hold the tension for three seconds and then relax.

⇨ Tense all the muscles in your waist, hold the tension for three seconds and then relax.

⇨ Tense all the muscles in your chest, hold the tension for three seconds and then relax.

⇨ Tense all the muscles in your arms, hold the tension for three seconds and then relax.

⇨ Tense all the muscles in your hands, hold the tension for three seconds and then relax.

⇨ Tense all the muscles in your shoulders, hold the tension for three seconds and then relax.

⇨ Tense all the muscles in your face (make the stupidest, stretchiest face imaginable!), hold the tension for three seconds and then relax.

All of the muscles in your body will now be completely relaxed and with it you should feel the tension, and the anxiety, ebb away.

Technique three: visualisation

So you've re-oxygenated your blood. Good. And you've relaxed every one of your muscles to relieve the tension in them. Good. Still feeling stressed? Don't worry. There's still one more technique you can try – visualisation.

Close your eyes (this might not be one to try on the bus!). Focus on clearing your mind for just five minutes. If a thought appears, don't ignore it. Visualise the thought being written on a piece of paper. Now imagine a deep lake in front of you. Screw the paper up, tie it to a stone, and drop it into the lake. Visualise it sinking through the still waters. Repeat this until you can feel your mind clearing. When you feel relaxed (and make no mistake, this will make you feel relaxed), open your eyes again.

This technique is a very basic form of meditation. You might have heard of meditation as something only Buddhists do to achieve enlightenment. In fact, it is something many people from all cultures practise to help focus their minds on whatever task they have at hand. And, as a bonus, it's incredibly relaxing, and a sure-fire way to beat anxiety. Try it now.

Have you tried each of the three techniques? Good. Now you're ready to begin.

REAL-LIFE EXAM TIPS

I always treat myself to a fancy hot chocolate with all the trimmings after an exam. This means I always have something to look forward to, however the exam goes.

MARY

REAL-LIFE EXAM TIPS

Whenever exams get you down, remind yourself that eventually you'll finish school and college, and you'll never have to do any exams ever again!

JEREMY

CHECKLIST

☐ *I know how to relax and I've practised relaxation techniques in different settings.*

☐ *I know that I can use these techniques when I feel anxiety building up.*

EXAM CHECK-UP

Have you:

❏ Worked out what kind of learner you are?

❏ Noted down the revision strategies that best suit your learning style?

❏ Got your exam timetable?

❏ Listed all of your subjects and all of your exams for each subject?

❏ Created your revision timetable?

❏ Designated your personal revision space?

❏ Relaxed?

Good. Then we can get down to the nitty-gritty of revision itself.

CHAPTER 9: ORGANISING YOUR NOTES: PART 1

It's highly likely that you are sitting at your desk right now with this chapter open in front of you. It's highly likely that all around you are stacks and piles and more stacks and even more piles of books – class books, anthologies, notebooks, novels, plays, textbooks, books about books. It's highly likely that you're thinking: 'Where am I supposed to start?' It's highly likely that your language was a little more colourful than mine just then.

These are the first things you should do:

Step one – Remember which subjects you have exams for

Consult your exam timetable and remind yourself of the subjects you have exams for. It is helpful to write these subjects down again to use as a tick list.

Step two – Make some space

Clear as many free spaces in your revision area as you can. These could be shelves, cupboards, drawers, or even places on the floor (as long as they're not going to be in your way every time you swivel on your chair or stand up to leave the room).

Step three – Create your Subject Zones

Designate each of the newly clear spaces for one of your exam subjects. These will be your Subject Zones. For example, this shelf is the English Subject Zone, this one above it is the Maths Subject Zone, this drawer is the Science Subject Zone, this part of the floor is the History Subject Zone, and so on. You can use your subject ticklist here to make sure you have created enough zones.

Step four – Fill your Subject Zones

Begin sifting through all the stacks and piles of books and all the loose leaves of paper or essays that you have. For each one, decide on which subject it is for, and place it in the Subject Zone you have created. Each time you come across a book that is for a subject you do not have exams for, place it on a separate pile.

Step five – Get rid of the unnecessary stuff

Once all books and notes and pieces of paper have been placed in their Subject Zones, pick up the separate pile of unnecessary books which you created in Step Four and carry it out of your revision space, putting it somewhere else in your home. You do not need this pile, so having it out of sight will help you to make your revision more manageable.

Step six – Reflect

Return to your revision space and look about at what you have created.

REAL-LIFE EXAM TIPS

My friends and I all studied Spanish together, so for a whole term before the exams we would watch a Spanish film together each Saturday night. We all ended up getting the highest marks in the class for our oral exams.

JAYNE

QUICK QUIZ – *Are you a messy or a tidy person?*

Q1 – *My bedroom is:*
a Messy
b Tidy

Answers

⇨ If you answered A you are a messy person.

⇨ If you answered B you are a tidy person.

There's plenty of debate about whether or not tidiness helps or messiness hinders. Looking now at your newly designed revision space with all its Subject Zones, you will be able to see at a glance if it's truly tidy or truly messy. Those tidies among you will have carefully rendered Subject Zones, perhaps with books stacked neatly and all facing in the same direction, perhaps with the biggest book at the bottom of a pile and the smallest at the top, perhaps even with a Post-it note above or next to each zone which clearly states which subject it is for.

And those messies among you will have fairly riotous Subject Zones, perhaps with books just thrown in haphazardly regardless of size or weight, perhaps with stacks which are already beginning to teeter to the left under their own weight, perhaps with a lot of Subject Zones relegated to the carpet.

The truth is, it doesn't matter for your revision whether you are tidy or messy. You have to find what works best for YOU.

Tidies tend to work best in areas that are free of clutter – this can help them, in turn, to keep their minds free of clutter and to work without having to worry about their surroundings. Messies, on the other hand, can sometimes revel in a bit of a mess. Have you ever said or heard a friend say: 'My mum cleaned my room. Now I don't know where anything is'? Even in a mess, logic can be found and messies often take solace in that. What matters is that your revision space is organised, and by creating your Subject Zones (whether they themselves are messy or tidy) you have done just that. Now you know where everything is when you need to revise it. Learning – and, with it, revision – can be done in both messy and tidy environments... but it is always done best in an organised environment.

REAL-LIFE EXAM TIPS

At the start of study leave I'd get up late and not start my revision until the afternoon. I realised pretty quickly that I wasn't getting nearly enough done, so I made a real effort to get up as if I had school and start revising no later than 9 a.m. I was much more motivated in the morning and got loads more done that way.

SEAN

REAL-LIFE EXAM TIPS

I found that association by smell worked for me. By wearing a different scent for each subject and blasting my revision notes with the same smell, I was able to sniff my sleeve during the exam and a lot came flooding back. To this day I can't smell jasmine and bergamot without thinking about the cognitive theories in psychology.

GRACE

CHECKLIST

❑ *I have separated my revision space into Subject Zones.*

❑ *I have filled each of my Subject Zones.*

❑ *I have decided whether I am a tidy or a messy person.*

CHAPTER 10: ORGANISING YOUR NOTES: PART 2

Now let's take a look at your individual Subject Zones. They might be inherently messy or tidy, but it is important that they are organised, too.

This chapter won't look at all your Subject Zones – each of you reading this book will have different subjects that you are about to take exams for. So, instead, let's just focus on one case study – one Subject Zone – and look at how you can organise that. Once we've gone through how to organise the subject below, you will be able to apply the techniques and skills you have learnt to your other Subject Zones.

Our case study will be GCSE English, as it is very likely that you will be taking this in the future or, if you are revising for your AS or A levels, that you have taken it in the past. It's a good case study for us to use, as it will be familiar to us all.

You've made a lot of lists so far, so this time we're going to try something different. We're going to make a mind map. First, you need to find a blank piece of paper. A3 is best but can be difficult to get hold of. A4 will do, but try not to go any smaller if you can help it.

Next, draw a box in the centre of the page and in that box write 'English', like this:

It might look something like this:

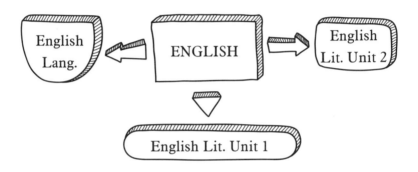

Most GCSE English exams are split into two separate sections. If you're not sure what they are, find out. Ask a friend (who might know) or ask your teacher (who will definitely know). If you're at home at the moment and can't get in touch with either your friends or your teacher, you should be able to find out with a quick bit of online research. Check out your school's website – they should have the information on there. At the very least, it will tell you which exam boards your school uses. It will probably be one of the following five:

AQA, Edexcel, WJEC, OCR, SQA

Once you know which exam board your school uses for English, a quick Google search will show you what sections to expect in each of your exams.

Now that you have that information, add it to your mind map, like this:

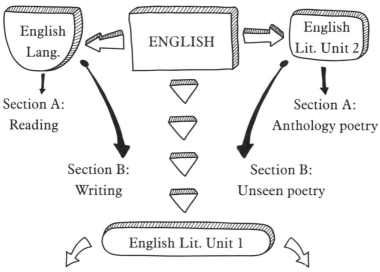

Now here comes the tricky part. Next to each of the latest branches you have added to your mind map (the sections, i.e. Section B: Exploring cultures), I want you to include as many things as you can think of that you associate with that section. Don't worry if you can't think of them all – you can always ask a teacher for help later – but start to include anything which you think is relevant. Once you begin, you'll be surprised at how many things you can think of.

Here are some ideas for you:

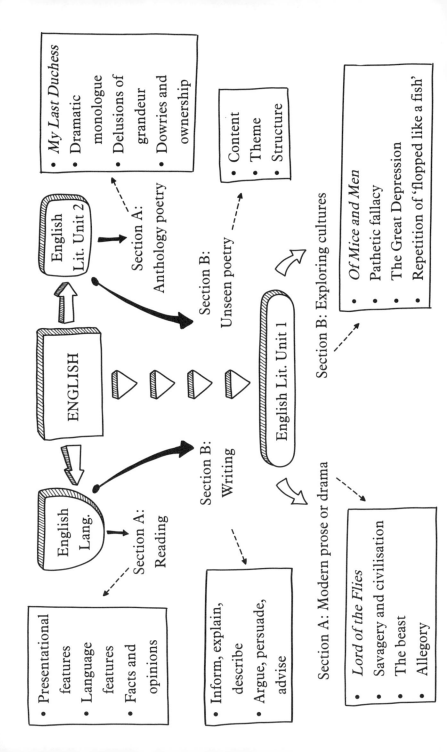

ENGLISH

English Lang.

Section A: Reading
- Presentational features
- Language features
- Facts and opinions

Section B: Writing
- Inform, explain, describe
- Argue, persuade, advise

English Lit. Unit 2

Section A: Anthology poetry
- *My Last Duchess*
- Dramatic monologue
- Delusions of grandeur
- Dowries and ownership

Section B: Unseen poetry
- Content
- Theme
- Structure

English Lit. Unit 1

Section B: Exploring cultures
- *Of Mice and Men*
- Pathetic fallacy
- The Great Depression
- Repetition of 'flopped like a fish'

Section A: Modern prose or drama
- *Lord of the Flies*
- Savagery and civilisation
- The beast
- Allegory

These are just some ideas. It's likely you will have many more. Try to fill your mind map with as many ideas as you can.

Do not throw away this mind map. It will be an invaluable revision tool for you as you get closer and closer towards your exams. Don't treat it as finished, either – you can always add more as you revise more and remember more.

However, your mind map is already invaluable – as it shows you exactly how your subject (in this case English) is split up into different exams and what each of those exams will require you to know and understand. Using your mind map as a guide, I now want you to go through all of the books and notes and pieces of paper in your English Subject Zone. Every time you come across something that is relevant to anything you have noted down on your mind map, organise it accordingly so that your notes are arranged into the different exams you are going to take for English and the different sections within each exam.

Organising your notes in this way will be a massive help for you as you revise. Remember, we've already established that you should approach your revision in small, achievable chunks. If you sit down one Tuesday morning and decide: 'Today, I'm going to revise English all day', it will not be the easiest day of your revision. If, however, you sit down on the same Tuesday morning and decide: 'Today, I'm going to revise English Literature Unit 2: Section B for 40 minutes, take a 20-minute break, then revise Maths Paper 1: Section A, then take a 20-minute break...' and so on and so on, you will inevitably have a much more productive revision session.

REAL-LIFE EXAM TIPS

If I need to remember a specific fact or statistic, or something word-for-word, I always use an acronym or mnemonic to help me. Condensing a long sentence or paragraph down to something short and catchy really helps it stick in my mind.

JENNY

TOP TIPS FOR ORGANISATION

When organising your subject notes into sections, remember that they are YOUR notes, and that you can organise them as you see fit. Rearrange them if they're not in the right order for you. Cardboard folders, polyfiles and ring binders with separate sections are all good ways of splitting up and rearranging your notes to make them more manageable.

REAL-LIFE EXAM TIPS

When I was revising for exams, I used to cover every surface of my bedroom in Post-it notes, using different colours for different subjects. It really helped me to remember things, because wherever I looked, there was always a fact in front of me.

ALASTAIR

This organisation might take you a few minutes, so I'm going to have a quick break while you do it.

All done? Good. Now I think you deserve a quick break. See you in ten minutes.

All done? Feeling better? Good. Because you've got a mammoth task ahead of you now. I want you to do exactly what you've just done for English for all of your other subjects. Here's a quick reminder of the steps to take for each subject:

01 Get a blank piece of paper.

02 Draw a box in the centre with the subject name inside it.

03 Consult your exam timetable and add each exam you will have for that subject onto your mind map.

04 Find out if each exam is split into sections (not all exams are). Add these sections to your mind map.

05 Next to each section, note down all the things you associate with that particular area of the subject.

06 Using your completed mind map, organise your Subject Zone so that your notes are arranged into each exam or exam section.

07 Repeat for the next subject.

Good luck! And see you in the next chapter!

CHECKLIST

☐ *I know which exam boards my school uses for each of my exam subjects.*

☐ *I have created my mind map for English (ignore if you do not have an English exam).*

☐ *I have created mind maps for all of my other exam subjects.*

REAL-LIFE EXAM STORIES: ALAN

At my school, once we came back after the Easter holidays in Year 11, it was like everything just completely changed. I had quite a small circle of friends, seven or eight of us, and suddenly none of them wanted to do anything except revise. I would ask each of them what they were up to after school or at the weekend and whether they wanted to hang out, and the answer was always the same: *I can't, I'm revising*.

I was revising too, but not nearly so much as the rest of them. I put it down to the fact that I was pretty mediocre academically – my grades tended to be the lowest in the group. But then one day Jimmy asked me what I was getting for passing my GCSEs.

I told him the truth: nothing.

'Isn't your mum rewarding you?' he asked. 'For each GCSE I get, my parents are getting me a new computer game.'

So that was why he was so motivated! I asked about some of the others, and it seemed that all of them had also struck some sort of deal with their parents. Olly's dad was going to start teaching him to drive if he passed more than five GCSEs. Marcus was getting a brand new phone just for turning up to every one of his exams. Luke (and I couldn't believe this one) was promised £100 for each exam he passed!

'You should ask your mum for a reward for doing your exams,' Jimmy said. 'It'll really help motivate you to revise. It's definitely helped me.'

Of course it has, I thought. *Just like new computer games or a phone or driving lessons or hundreds of pounds would definitely motivate me too*. But I already knew my mum could not afford any of that. A single parent with only a part-time job, she just didn't have that kind of money. Over dinner that night, I was a bit depressed and quiet, and when my mum asked me what was wrong, I told her the truth.

'You're right, I can't afford any of those things,' she said. 'But maybe there's something else I can get you if you pass all your exams. Maybe something you've always wanted. Maybe something that you don't buy, but something you rescue... something that you re-home ...'

I wolfed my dinner down, went straight to my bedroom and began revising immediately.

'You'll have to walk it every day!' my mum called up the stairs.

She had found exactly the right way to motivate me. I had wanted a dog for as long as I could remember, but my mum had always come up with some reason why we couldn't. Over the following weeks, I spent every spare moment revising, and when I needed a short break I would visit the local rescue home's website. When I needed a long break, I would visit the rescue home itself.

Needless to say, I passed all of my exams, and I've no doubt that I passed them because I had the motivation to revise. My mum couldn't afford much, but it turns out that what I needed to motivate me was free to a good home anyway.

CHAPTER 11:
WIDER READING

As we've already said in an earlier chapter, you should try to read around your subject as much as you possibly can. First, it is very important to work out which books are your core texts (again, if you're ever unsure, just ask your teacher). These are the books you will have studied in class, the books that whole lessons will have revolved around, the books that will have been given to you to take home (and take care of), the books that you've probably read over and over again already.

Before we move on, I'd just like to check that you've identified your core texts, and that you've placed them in the correct Subject Zones of your revision space. If you haven't, do that now.

Once you have, we can get on to what this chapter is all about – that you shouldn't just rely on these core texts. Of course, they will give you an excellent grounding in the knowledge you need to acquire, and they should definitely be consulted regularly, but if you truly want those top grades, you're going to have to push your reading and research beyond the barriers of those core texts.

In English, for example, a good answer to an exam question will:

01 Answer the question given (and if that sounds obvious, it is, but you'll be surprised by just how many candidates either go off on wild tangents or simply list all their knowledge rather than sticking to what the question has asked for).

02 Know and understand the subject material well.

03 Be able to discuss and analyse the subject material effectively.

04 Embed quotations in the answer and then explain them sufficiently to refer back to the question.

REAL-LIFE EXAM TIPS

In some of my exams (especially for subjects like the humanities), I had to write essays, and I knew fairly well what they would ask me to write about, so I would plan out a range of essays before entering the exam. Even if I didn't get exactly the question I had predicted, I was able to borrow from the plans I had memorised and hit the ground running.

HARRY

A really good answer, on the other hand, will do all of the above, but it will also show off to the examiner that the candidate has read around their subject – and make no mistake, showing off is a good thing to do in exams. Many of us don't like to show off in public. It makes us look arrogant; it makes us look self-centred. But your examiners want you to show off your knowledge, so don't be afraid to do so.

English isn't the only subject in which you can read around your core texts. Every subject provides opportunities for you to widen your knowledge and show off to the examiner that you know more than they think you might. This is what examiners call context, and it shows them that you've gone the extra mile to learn about and truly understand your subject.

If we were to list all the extra texts you could read for every single exam for every single exam board for every single subject for every single school in the UK, it would fill another book. So we won't do that now. What we will do is suggest that you have a chat with your teachers. Remember, these are people who have devoted their working lives to learning the subjects you are about to take exams for. They have amassed so much knowledge on the subjects that, to be honest, they'll probably be relieved to advise you on the extra material you should read and why.

If you're stuck for ideas on how to read widely, just follow some of the handy tips below.

IDEAS FOR WIDER READING

⇨   Look in the back of your core texts. Most of them will have endnotes, bibliographies and suggestions for further reading. These can be ideal places to conduct your extra research. If the author of the book you're studying read and relied upon them, it's a good bet that you can read and rely upon them too.

⇨   Go onto Amazon and type the keywords of the topic you are studying. Amazon promotes itself as the place to find every single book ever published, so you will probably be presented with thousands upon thousands of books. Don't worry – you don't need to read them all! The great thing about Amazon is that it ranks the books in order of how popular and relevant they are to your search requirements. Look through the first ten and try to work out if any will be helpful to you – clicking on them and reading the product descriptions and customer reviews is a good way of finding out if they're the right books for your revision.

⇨ In most cases, you won't need to buy these books. Note down or print off your refined list (i.e., the top ten books that appeared in your search) and take it to your local library. If they don't have them in stock, there's a good chance they'll order at least one in for you if you can convince them it's a worthy read (this is where your use of the library as a revision space will definitely pay off!).

⇨ While you're in the library, have a chat with the librarians. They are trained to know their stock well, and will be able to give you great advice on some other books to check out.

⇨ Have a look for any podcasts that might be available about the subject you are revising. Online sound libraries like iTunes are filled with great podcasts where people who know certain subjects intimately talk about them at length.

⇨ Talk to members of your family. Don't forget that they once took exams, too. They might have books they can lend you but – more importantly – they might simply be able to talk to you about the topic and offer you crucial insights which you hadn't realised before, and which you can use in your exams.

> ⇨ As I said earlier, talk to your teachers as well. They will have plenty of information to offer you about the subject, but I guarantee that they'll also have a spare book or two lurking on their shelves. Ask them nicely enough and they'll probably lend it to you – on the condition that it comes back to them in pristine condition, of course!

There is one other way you can search for extra information about your topic or subject. That way is by using the Internet. But a careful use of the Internet demands a whole chapter in itself – the very next chapter, in fact.

CHECKLIST

☐ *I have worked out which books are my core texts for each exam.*

☐ *I understand that I need to read more than just these core texts so that I can give my exam answers context.*

☐ *I have researched the different books I can read.*

☐ *I have found at least one extra book for each subject I am taking.*

CHAPTER 12:
USING THE INTERNET

Before we begin this chapter, let's just have a quick look at how you currently use the Internet. Below is a list of some of the most popular websites today. Once you've read through them all, rank them by placing numbers in the middle column (one being the website you use the most each week, 17 being the website you use the least each week). Then, once you've done that, try to work out how much time (in hours) you spend on each website each week, and note down the total in the right-hand column. (HINT: Don't just include the time you spend on the websites on your computer, but also take into account how long you spend on the apps on your smartphone or tablet.)

Website	Rank	Hours I spend per week
Facebook		
Twitter		
YouTube		
Wikipedia		
Email		
iTunes		
Pinterest		
BBC		
Amazon		
Reddit		
Online games		

eBay		
Tumblr		
Snapchat		
WhatsApp		
BuzzFeed		
Others		

We're not going to rate these websites in any kind of order in which you should be using them; this is merely an exercise for you to assess how much time you spend on each. If the time you spend on sites such as Facebook or online games vastly outweighs the time you spend on the BBC website, for example, then you are completely normal. Social networking sites generate so many hits from their users because they employ a whole array of subtle techniques that keep you coming back for more. Informational websites (such as news websites like the BBC), on the other hand, do not use such tricks and their overall hits suffer as a result.

The fact is, most people access a social networking site more regularly than they access an informational site. But, right now, you are not most people; while everyone else can use their online hours for entertainment, you should be using yours for revision.

The key thing to remember is that this is not going to last. You don't have to delete your Facebook or Twitter accounts, you don't have to cut out your Snapchats or WhatsApp conversations altogether; you don't have to give it all up in one fell swoop.

What you do have to do, though, is cut down.

Once all this is over, once you've completed that crucial final exam, you can go back to your old Internet-browsing habits. But, right now, you're in a rather unique position – you are revising for your exams. And when you revise for your exams, the Internet can be both a saviour and a curse.

Did you know that 82 per cent of all statistics on the Internet are made up? You probably didn't. Because I just made up that statistic.

The big difference between the material you find on the Internet and the material you find in books is one we call 'verification'. To 'verify' something is to make absolutely sure that it is the truth. While all books must go through the process of verification (in that the publishers have to check that all the facts the authors have included are indeed true), websites aren't subject to the same rules.

Anyone can write anything on the Internet and pass it off as truth. And, as long as it's presented in a professional design, it's very easy to believe that it is indeed the truth.

Quick quiz

Here are ten 'facts' that I've just found through a quick online search. Can you spot which ones are true and which are made up?

01 Eighty per cent of men over the age of 80 have prostate cancer.

02 Regular shaving increases your stubble.

03 The winner of a game show called *Find the Weasel* found a weasel among 81 ferrets.

04 The winner of a game show called *Touch the Truck* stood touching a truck for 81 hours.

05 Dinosaurs used to have feathers.

06 If you stood every living human shoulder to shoulder, they would fit on the Isle of Wight.

07 People who live in London are never more than six feet away from a rat.

08 The Queen owns one sixth of the Earth's land surface.

09 Cows have four stomachs.

10 Octopuses have three hearts.

Before you check out the answers on the next page, ask yourself this: how many of these 'facts' would you have believed if you'd read them on a website? All of them? None of them? Some of them?

Unfortunately, many of us choose to believe facts such as these simply because they have been written down and presented to us in a professional format. We are conditioned to think this way because books are a reliable source of information.

Long before the Internet existed, most people got their information about the world from the books they read. And, when they read them, they therefore started to believe that everything they read was true because, as I said before, all books need to be fact checked before they can go to print. Sadly, much of the Internet has taken advantage of this – the creators of some websites know that we have been conditioned to believe everything we read, and so they've presented their information in such a way as to make us believe that it is true, even if it's not.

Consider the above ten 'facts'. They have been presented to you in such a way as to make you believe them. And, if I hadn't already written that some of them were indeed false, would you have taken them all as true just because you'd read them? Perhaps. Perhaps not. It's up to you to decide.

Nevertheless, here are the answers. How did you do?

01 True

02 False

03 False

04 True

05 True

06 False

07 False

08 True

09 False

10 True

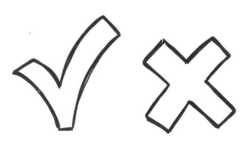

Internet safety

You've probably had lessons in school about Internet safety. You've probably had whole modules of PSHE or Citizenship about how to make sure that when you use the Internet, you use it as safely as possible.

What you will have learnt in those lessons is extremely valuable. The Internet is a brilliant thing – it has connected people across the world in ways that telephone lines, the Royal Mail and even television cannot ever come close to. It is a massive and continually growing source of information which is so easy to use: you can look at an aerial view of Papua New Guinea or contact people on the other side of the world from you in just a few seconds, or find out the latest goings-on in New York at just the click of a button.

However, it goes without saying that, for all its brilliance, it can also be a very dangerous place. I once read a statistic that Google can direct you to only 0.2 per cent of what is on the Internet. We already know that statistics we find online (which is where I found this one) can't always be trusted, but whether it's true or not, it's a very important point. There are a lot of dark places lurking on the Internet – and many of them don't want to be found by the likes of you and me.

The dangers of the Internet

So you probably already know from your PSHE or Citizenship lessons how you should and shouldn't use the Internet. You probably already know that if you share an intimate photograph on Facebook you'll be offering that photograph out to the whole world and not just your friends. You probably already know that if you reveal information about yourself such as your bank details or your family history, that information can easily be found by people you wouldn't necessarily want to find it. You probably already know that there are people out there who use the Internet for bad purposes, such as identity theft and cyber bullying.

If you don't already know about these things, please make an effort to find out soon. It's an incredibly important part of being a safe user of the Internet.

What's this got to do with revision?

This is the kind of stuff you need to be aware of when social networking, for example, or when shopping online or playing online games. But, surely, using the Internet for revision purposes is simply a search for information and what can go wrong with that?

The answer is that a lot can go wrong with that. There aren't just bad people on the Internet, there is also bad information and it can get through to you when you least expect it. You've probably heard plenty of stories about people (and not just young people – this can happen to anyone) who have begun communicating with someone else on the Internet – perhaps through a forum or chat room or even Facebook – and that person has turned out to not be who they pretended to be. The same thing can happen with information. Some 'facts' are dressed up and made to look like real facts even if they are not, but they have been written so convincingly that it can often be hard to tell the difference.

Why bad information can harm your revision

When you use the Internet to find information about the subject you are studying, you should always tread carefully. Be assured: if you note down a wrong 'fact' which you've found on the Internet, and then use it in an exam, the examiner will spot it. Most examiners are teachers and they know the subjects of the exams that they are marking like the back of their hand. If something pops up in an exam answer that looks like it might be false, they will check it. And, if it turns out to actually be false, you won't get the vital marks that you need to achieve the brilliant grades you're after.

REMINDER: *It is important here to revisit something we learnt very early on in this book. An examiner will never deduct marks for a wrong answer. However, if your answer is wrong, you won't gain the marks for it that a correct answer would give you. And these are the marks that could be the difference between a poor grade and a good grade in your exam, and in your final grade.*

During your exams, you will be set very strict time limits. These time limits have been devised by the person who wrote the exam to give you just enough time to get 100 per cent, but not a moment more. So, when it comes to your exams, you need to make sure you have the exact amount of good information necessary to get as close to that 100 per cent as possible.

In your revision time, however, you have a little more luxury – so make the most of it. Use your time to make sure that everything you research on the Internet will be of use to you in your exams and that none of it is worthless information.

This can seem daunting at first, but don't worry. In the next chapter, we've provided some guidelines that will help you to ensure your Internet research will always give you the results you need. Have a read through them, stick to them during your revision and you won't go wrong.

CHECKLIST

❑ I have assessed how I currently use the Internet.

❑ I have decided to cut down on using websites that don't help with my revision.

❑ I know that if I find some information on the Internet, it does not automatically make that piece of information a fact.

❑ I understand the importance of staying safe online.

❑ I know that not all the information I find on the Internet will help me in my exams.

❑ I know that only the <u>good</u> information I find on the Internet will help me in my exams.

CHAPTER 13:
HOW TO SPOT IF A FACT IS ACTUALLY A FACT

There are times when you just know that a 'fact' is utter nonsense and there are times when you just know that it's true (perhaps your teacher has already told you it or you've read it in one of your core texts). For all those times in between, for all those times when you're just not sure, try out one or two of these ideas:

⇨ Can you find the same 'fact' (or, at least, something very similar) on at least three other websites? (This doesn't take as much effort as you might think. Simply copy and paste the 'fact' into Google. The page at the top of the list will probably be the one where you found the 'fact' in the first place, but scroll down through the rest of the results on the page. Do other websites look like they also have the same 'fact' – or, at least, as we've said, something similar?)

⇨ Check your books – both your core texts and your class books. If you're doing some wider reading then you may not find what you're looking for, but you never know what you might have noted down during a lesson.

How to get TOP GRADES in your exams

⇨ Ask your teacher, or your parents, or anyone else who you suspect might be knowledgeable on the subject. Maybe your aunty has a love of Geography and can help you sort the truth from the lies; maybe your grandad knows the ins and outs of electric circuitry; maybe your next-door neighbour speaks fluent French. You won't know until you ask!

⇨ Research the website where you found the information. Again, this isn't difficult. Simply type the name of the website into Google. Once more, the first search result will probably be the website itself, but if that website has a reputation for being a dodgy source of knowledge then there will be plenty of other results that show it up for what it really is.

⇨ Always try to use websites that have a good reputation. Admittedly, it can be difficult to spot which are reliable and which are not. These days, anyone with a laptop and a bit of spare time can create even the most professional-looking website. So, if you're not sure about the website you're looking at, here are a couple of tips that might make you want to be just a little suspicious.

TOP TIPS FOR SPOTTING AN UNTRUSTWORTHY WEBSITE

⇨ Ignore most websites that end in geocities.com.

⇨ Also ignore most websites that have a person's name in the URL.

⇨ Any website that has a fluorescent green background (or any fluorescent colour, for that matter) is probably best avoided.

⇨ Also avoid any website that is written entirely in Comic Sans, or CAPITALS, or uses more than one punctuation mark at the end of a sentence!!??!!??

⇨ If you spot the words 'conspiracy theory', you should probably move on. Any sentence that begins with the words, 'People claim this is a conspiracy theory, but...' is not likely to tell you a fact. It is more likely to tell you a rubbish conspiracy theory (in much the same way as any sentence that begins with the words, 'I'm not racist, but...' is only likely to then say something very racist indeed).

REAL-LIFE EXAM TIPS

I found that one of the most useful resources I had was the clock function on my phone. I used the stopwatch to time myself sitting practice papers, I used the alarm to let me know when each revision session should begin and end, and I used the reminders to flash up quick test questions (which I had typed in) at random times throughout each day.

LYRA

So that's the untrustworthy websites dealt with. But what about the ones you can trust? There are plenty out there – in the same way that there are plenty of people on the Internet who don't want to deceive you or lie to you or get you to believe something that just isn't true. However, if you want a quick list of a few that come with the Top Grades in Exams seal of approval, then read on.

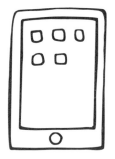

Five great revision websites

⇨ **www.bbc.co.uk/education** is the new URL for the classic BBC Bitesize revision website, which has been helping students revise for years. They don't come much better than this.

⇨ **www.s-cool.co.uk** is handy if you can't find what you're looking for on Bitesize. It covers most subjects at GCSE and A level.

⇨ **www.getrevising.co.uk** is helpful for organising your time and chatting to other like-minded students about any exam-based issues you might be facing.

⇨ **www.examsolutions.net** is great purely for Maths revision.

⇨ Finally, **www.bbc.co.uk** is the main BBC website and it's a great place to find up-to-date information about the world which can stand you in great stead for your exams.

The great Wikipedia debate

Wikipedia is the largest ever collection of human knowledge compiled in one place. An online encyclopedia which is constantly growing and tries to cover every single subject you could ever possibly think of, it really is a marvel of technology.

However, its strength is also its curse. Wikipedia has been so successful because it allows anyone to contribute an article to the website. This means that it can reach the most outer limits of human knowledge. It doesn't just rely on the limited efforts of a few university professors; instead, it has the combined wisdom of everyone who knows anything about anything.

But this is also its downfall. Because anyone can submit anything to it. That means that a lot of the information you can find on Wikipedia hasn't been checked (in fairness, Wikipedia does try to weed out articles and information that turn out to be false), but there are still plenty of articles on there that don't even come close to the truth. Because Wikipedia is so widely used and so often referred to, it can look like everything on there is official and verified – but this is not always the case.

The fact is, Wikipedia can be very helpful to you when you're trying out some wider reading around your subject, but you should be very careful with the information you find. Always go through the bullet points listed at the start of this chapter with anything you find on Wikipedia. Most of the time, you'll realise that you have discovered something truthful – but for those times when you have discovered something made up, the bullet points above can help to ensure that you don't bring these into your exams.

So, in conclusion, use Wikipedia, but use it with a healthy dose of scepticism. And if you're not sure what 'scepticism' means, you can Wikipedia it. It's all right, I've checked: it's got that one right.

CHECKLIST

❑ *I know how to check up on whether or not a website is telling me the truth.*

❑ *I know which websites to ignore (perhaps make a list of ones you have come across).*

❑ *I know which websites to use (perhaps make a list of ones you like).*

❑ *I now know how to find <u>good</u> information on the Internet.*

REAL-LIFE EXAM STORIES: LAURA

I'm a scientist. That's what I do and that's who I am. Ever since I was little, I've approached life from a scientific angle. I like to test things, to see which approach is the best and most effective. That's how I know that tea tastes best when the bag has been left in for between two and two and a half minutes, or that a 2005 Vauxhall Vectra can hold 13 children of 12 years of age at average BMI. I once spent a whole year rigorously testing which colour of hair-dye provoked the nicest compliments from my friends and gave me the most self-confidence (if you're interested, it's auburn).

Like any good scientist, I experiment, measure, and observe, and I do so whenever I possibly can. Last year, I sat my GCSEs. I was determined to approach these with the same scientific method I apply to so much else. But the GCSEs themselves would be no time for experimentation. That would be too much of a risk. The experimentation (and the measuring and observing) would have to happen before the GCSEs, during my revision. And, if I could use my scientific method to find out the best way to approach an exam, that would surely help me to succeed when it came to the real thing.

First of all, I needed resources to work with, and so I asked each of my teachers for as many practice exam papers as they could spare. They seemed delighted by my request, and offered me more than I had anticipated. I started out small, searching for any differences that might arise from pen colour choice (none found) or planning an answer versus not planning an answer (planning an answer was more effective almost every time). Once I was warmed up with these, I set out to find the answer to something I had pondered for a long while.

All my teachers had told me that it was much more effective to revise steadily for an extended period of time rather than cramming the night before. But I had never been sure of this. Was that actually true? Or was it just something teachers said? Had they ever tested it themselves? I doubted they had. I would find out for myself.

I picked two subjects at random, chose two practice exam papers for each, arranged them into two groups, and then gave myself the time-period of five days. For the first three days, I revised for Group A of the practice exam papers. Then, on the fourth day (or the fourth evening, to be precise), I crammed for Group B. On the fifth day, I took all the exams in a random order. I recorded the results, and then repeated the experiment with two other subjects, recorded the results for them and then did it one final time with two more subjects.

There are times when you are conducting an experiment and its conclusion becomes clear long before you have finished. I knew it the second I sat down to complete the first set of practice papers. It was obvious how better-prepared I was for the 'revision' group than for the 'cramming' group. The results of the two groups of exams confirmed that this was the case. I continued with the experiment anyway because that's what a good scientist does, and each new set of results continued to prove what I already knew.

So there you go. Revising steadily for an extended period of time is more effective than cramming the night before. It's not just something your teachers tell you. It's science.

CHAPTER 14: PRACTISING YOUR EXAMS

Practising exams is one of the best revision methods out there. There's a reason why you take mocks before your real exams. There's a reason why your teachers are probably making you do practice paper after practice paper. And the reason is: it genuinely helps.

Think of something you're really good at. It can be anything – playing a particular computer game, cooking, playing a sport, writing stories, playing a musical instrument – anything at all. (And, if at this point, you're saying to yourself that you're not good at anything, think again – because you're wrong. We are all good at something. All that stuff I said in Chapter 2 about multiple intelligences should hopefully have made you realise that by now.)

Once you've decided what it is you are good at (if you're still really stuck, try to think of something you like doing – often, we like doing the things that we're good at), try to work out how much time you've spent doing that thing. It's very likely that you've devoted an awful lot of time to it. You're good at it because you've practised it. It's incredibly difficult to pick up a new skill straight away – everyone who is really good at something (including the most gifted athletes or singers or actors) is good at it because they've spent time on it: honing the skill, making sure that their body or mind or both are as attuned to doing the thing as brilliantly as possible.

It all comes down to a very simple statement. It might be simple, but it's absolutely true:

THE MORE YOU DO SOMETHING, THE BETTER YOU GET AT IT.

So let's apply that statement to exams. It stands to reason that the more you do exams, the better you get at them. This is one of the reasons why exams get more difficult the older you get. Sure, as you get older your brain grows and your intelligence increases and you become more capable of advanced learning – but when you come to take the exams for your university degree, it definitely helps that you've already sat your A level and GCSE exams. You will have practised taking exams, and the techniques, strategies and experience you will have gained from all this practice will help you extraordinarily in your new exams.

It is the truth that those people who spend more time practising their exams do better in the real thing than those people who don't. You may not realise it, but your school will have been helping you practise exams since you were 11 years old, or maybe even younger. You will probably have taken end-of-year exams every June or July since Year 6, and though these may have seemed at the time like they were set just to make your school life that little bit more difficult, actually they were there to make sure that, when it came to exams, you were practised.

Some of you, however, still might not be feeling ready. You might think that all those previous exams were nothing compared with what you're about to take. What if these are your first proper exams? What if you've never taken truly important exams like these before? What if you just don't feel like you've practised exams enough in the past?

If you are thinking this, there's no need to panic. Because you've still got time. As I said at the start of this chapter, practising exams is one of the best revision methods out there. That's the beauty of it – doing a practice exam counts as revision!

One crucial thing to remember is that it is never too early to start doing practice exams. In fact, the earlier the better. If you can practise each exam two, three or even four times, you'll be increasing your chances of achieving those brilliant grades in the real thing every single time.

Below are some steps to follow to make sure you are well and truly practised at taking exams. Even if you do feel you've got enough experience of them, I still sincerely suggest you follow these steps, as they will always help with your revision.

Step one – Find your revision timetable

Go into your revision space and look at the revision timetable you have pinned to the wall. Take it down and pick up a pen.

Step two – Allocate times

On your revision timetable, find one revision time for each of your subjects. Draw a star next to each of the times you have decided on. These stars will be the times when you will take your practice exams.

Step three – Ensure you have the right amount of practice exams

Try to make sure you do at least one practice exam for every real exam you will take – refer back to your exam timetable if you're unsure about this. (HINT: You don't have to do them all in one week. If you have enough time left before your exams, spread them out over a fortnight so that you're not taking a practice exam every hour.)

Step four – Get the papers

Go into school. Find each of your teachers and ask them for a practice exam paper for each of your upcoming exams. There's no need to be nervous about this. Trust me – if anything, it'll make you very popular with your teachers. Teachers love it when their students want to practise their exams, and they'll probably give you more papers than you want!

Step five – Get organised

Take all of the practice exam papers home and organise them into the order in which you will take them according to your revision timetable.

Step six – Get some writing paper

Make sure you've got plenty of spare paper to write on for when you take the practice exams. If you don't have enough, ask your tutor at school – as long as you tell them that it's for practice exams to help your revision, you'll be sure to receive plenty.

Step seven – Get in the right mindset

When it comes to your first practice exam, try to recreate the exam conditions as much as possible. This doesn't mean that you need to be sitting in a huge hall with 100 other people your age doing the same thing. In fact, you can do your practice exam just as well in your own private revision space. Read the front page of the exam paper. This will tell you how long you have for the exam and what you're allowed (for example, some Maths papers allow calculators whereas others don't). Stick to what the paper says. If it says you have 45 minutes to complete the exam, for example, then set yourself 45 minutes to do it and not a moment more.

Step eight – Turn everything off

Your revision space should always be a quiet area where you won't be interrupted, but you need to make doubly sure it is now. There will be no interruptions in your real exam, so make sure there are no interruptions for your practice exam, either. Turn all your devices off. Don't just put them on silent. Turn them off. In your real exam, you won't be allowed to consult your computer. In your real exam, you might be disqualified if your phone vibrates with an incoming text message or email or Facebook notification. So recreate those exam conditions in your revision space as best as you can.

Step nine – Practise!

Take the practice exam.

Step ten – Repeat!

Repeat Steps Six to Nine for each of your practice exams.

Step eleven – Repeat again!

If you've still got time before the real thing, do them all again. And again. Once you're absolutely sick of taking practice exams, that means you're ready for the real thing.

REAL-LIFE EXAM TIPS

One of my university lecturers gave me a piece of advice that changed my life. They said: 'I can only assume that you just have so much bubbling through your very active brain that you do NOT process the material as it comes out. You splurge everything you know but you do NOT actually answer the question!' The lecturer told me to focus on the actual question and not just to react to a trigger word. It really did help me focus on what the question actually was and what the most coherent answer would be.

ANDREW

REAL-LIFE EXAM TIPS

Read through the instructions and questions at least twice. It is so easy to panic when you get in there. Once, for a mock GCSE, I answered three questions from different parts of the paper and I ended up only getting marked on one 4-mark question... disaster!

AMY

REAL-LIFE EXAM TIPS

Always show your workings out in Maths/ Science exams, as you can often get some points for your method even if the answer is wrong.

CHLOË

REAL-LIFE EXAM TIPS

I had a really long bus journey between my house and the school – it took an hour each way! I didn't like the fact that I was wasting two hours of every day, but I've never been able to read on transport as it makes me feel sick. So I started recording voice memos of me reading through my notes, and then I would listen back to them on the bus.

CARL

CHECKLIST

❏ *I know that the more I do something, the better I will get at it.*

❏ *I have decided on the times when I will take a practice exam for each of my exam subjects.*

❏ *I have at least one practice exam paper for each of my exam subjects.*

❏ *I have taken each practice exam in my revision space under exam conditions.*

CHAPTER 15: MARKING YOUR PRACTICE EXAMS

It is perhaps important to begin this chapter by telling you that taking practice exams is a great revision exercise in itself. It will help you get in the right frame of mind; it will help you get better at writing under timed conditions; and it will help you prepare for the kind of questions you might get asked in your real exams.

You don't always need to have the answers you write for your practice exams checked. In fact, sometimes you might feel you've done terribly in the practice and don't actually want anyone to see what you've written. Maybe you froze. Maybe you couldn't write more than two sentences. If this has happened to you while doing a practice exam, you should know that this is actually a good thing. Imagine if you hadn't practised. Imagine if you'd gone into your real exam and you'd frozen then, or you'd not been able to write more than two sentences! This can happen, but more often than not it happens to those people who don't practise. Now that you have practised, you will know if this is the kind of thing that might happen to you, and you will know to spend more time revising that subject to make sure it definitely doesn't happen during the real exam.

Remember what I said in the last chapter:

THE MORE YOU DO SOMETHING, THE BETTER YOU GET AT IT.

If you've just taken a practice exam and sat for the best part of 30 minutes twiddling your thumbs, there is nothing wrong with that – because you've still got time. You've still got time to revise some more and take the practice exam again. And then you've still got time to revise even more after that, and maybe take it once more. If you follow this process, by the time you get to your real exams you'll know exactly what it is you have to face, and you will have the knowledge and skills at hand to make sure you ace them.

Nevertheless, it can be very helpful to check over your answers for a practice exam or get someone else to check over them for you.

REAL-LIFE EXAM TIPS

I would revise right through the day, but I never revised after dinner. I needed to have some down-time before I went to bed, otherwise my head would be reeling from it all and I wouldn't be able to sleep.

DEBBIE

Feedback – whether it's from a teacher or your parents or your best friend – can be really valuable, and if you don't mind showing your answers to someone else it can be a great way of learning what you've done well and what targets for improvement you might still have.

Unsure of where to start? Perhaps try some of these:

Your teachers

You probably adore some of your teachers. You probably find some others not quite to your taste. Either way, never forget that part of a teacher's job is to help you make sure that you get the best possible grade you can for your exams. And your teachers, whether you like them or not, will be extremely encouraging if they know you've taken some practice exams all by yourself.

You should probably also not forget that your teachers are as busy as you are at the moment – so, while they will love that you've taken it upon yourself to practise your exams, they just may not have the time to mark your answers for you. However, many of your teachers will gladly mark your answers for you, grade them and also give you advice on how to improve your grades. The key thing to remember is that it doesn't hurt to ask. Even if they don't have the time, you will certainly go up in their estimation for using your initiative.

Your parents

While your parents may not quite understand the finer points of how to assess an exam-style answer, they can still definitely help you. Don't forget that they probably took very similar exams to yours when they were your age, and they will have their own tips and advice on how to do brilliantly. Maybe they can check over your spelling, punctuation and grammar; maybe they can offer extra ideas for you to use which you hadn't thought of yourself; maybe they can help you research something further so that you've got the kind of understanding you need to ensure that, when you take the real exam, you'll get that fantastic grade you crave. Either way, just like your teachers, they will be hugely impressed that you've taken the time to practise your exams, and scoring brownie points with your parents never hurts when, later on, you want that new game or phone or, dare I say it, car…

Your friends

I've said it before and I'll say it again. Your friends are going through exactly the same situation that you are going through right now. So use that. You've probably done peer marking or peer assessment in lessons before, right? The reason you did it was because sometimes, when we learn, our 'peers' (people of our own age group) can help us understand the things we've learnt better than our teachers can. Have you ever discussed a problem with a mate (and not necessarily a problem to do with exams, but maybe something to do with your social life or any of the ways in which you're finding being a young adult difficult), and together you've found a solution to the problem? In fact, has just talking about it with a friend made you feel better? You can apply the same thing to revision and to exams.

One great idea is to decide with a friend that you're both going to take the same practice exam paper separately. Then, once you've completed it, get together and share your answers. Talking about the exam paper with each other can be a wonderful way of realising what you've both done well and what you both could do better, and it's also a nice excuse for meeting up with a friend during a time when you might be stuck on your own in your revision space for days on end.

Your older brothers and/or sisters (if you have them)

If you do have older brothers and/or sisters, it's likely they went to the same school as you. It's likely they took exactly the same exams as you just a few years ago. It's likely they did the same revision. It's likely that, when they got their results, they found out what they did well and what they could have improved upon. Have a chat with them, use their knowledge and employ it within your own revision to make sure you do even better than them.

Yourself

When you write something, it can be very difficult to work out what's good about it and what's not so good. When you write something, because you're using your words and your ideas and your thoughts, you can become very personally involved in it, and it can be difficult to see where you've done well and where you might have not done so well.

Nevertheless, there are still things you can do to improve your work. First of all, once you've finished your practice exam, take a ten-minute break. Then, come back to what you've written and read back through it as slowly and as carefully as you can. Can you spot anything that immediately jumps out at you? Maybe you've missed a full stop, or you've forgotten to insert a paragraph, or you haven't shown your working, or you've forgotten to add a conclusion. These are all things that can be very easy to miss while you're writing. Taking a break and coming back to your work with fresh eyes can help you look over your work with a clearer mind. (HINT: Sometimes it can help to read your work aloud. This might be a bit embarrassing at first, so check the house to make sure no one can hear you. Then read it to yourself in your normal speaking voice, without whispering. This is a very effective way of spotting any mistakes you might have made which a silent read-through could miss.)

If you can, try to get the mark schemes for your upcoming exams from your teachers. Most teachers use these in their planning in the run-up to exams, so it's likely that you have them glued into your class books already. Use the mark schemes to check through your work and, if you're feeling confident enough, to grade it. It might all seem like gibberish at first glance (and don't worry if it does – your teachers probably feel the same way!), but highlighting keywords in the mark scheme's criteria can help you understand what the examiners are looking for. And, once again, if you're ever unsure of what something means, ask your teacher. They will be able to explain the mark scheme so that it makes sense to you. Self-grading your practice exam answers is a brilliant way of knowing how to improve your work. You'll be putting yourself in the examiners' shoes – when you know what they're looking for, you'll also know how to give it to them in the real thing.

CHECKLIST

☐ *My teachers.*

☐ *My parents.*

☐ *My friends.*

☐ *My older brothers and/or sisters.*

☐ *I have found the mark schemes for my exams.*

☐ *I have marked my own exam-style answers.*

EXAM CHECK-UP

Have you:

☐ Created your Subject Zones?

☐ Organised all your notes?

☐ Created your mind map for each of your exam subjects?

☐ Identified your core texts?

☐ Reread your core texts?

☐ Read around your core texts?

☐ Assessed how you currently use the Internet?

☐ Decided which websites you should spend most of your time on while revising?

☐ Taken a practice paper for each of your exams?

☐ Found someone who can help you mark your answers?

☐ Got the mark schemes for your exams?

☐ Used the mark schemes to mark your own answers?

Good. Then it's time to tackle the exams themselves.

REAL-LIFE EXAM STORIES: SHANE

Being the oldest sibling isn't easy. If you've got younger brothers and sisters you'll know exactly what I mean. And if you haven't, you're welcome to step into my shoes for a while and see what it's like. Because I've got it extreme – I'm the oldest of five.

All right, so I have to admit that the respect is pretty good. Because you're the oldest, all the rest automatically look up to you. But that also means you've got to set a good example. I've always tried to. As much as I tease and fight with my younger brothers and sisters, I still love them, and I like to think that, so far, my life has served as a good inspiration for all of them.

I think I realised it most when it came to my GCSEs. I was determined to do well in them – to set a good example. I knew full well that to get good grades I'd have to put in the hours revising, and I was prepared to do that. At school, I worked through my free periods and through the second half of each lunch break. The real problem came when I was at home.

That's the other problem with being the oldest of five. When you're 16 years old and there're four people younger than you living in the same house, it can get seriously noisy. In fact, it doesn't just *get* seriously noisy, it *is* seriously noisy, all the time. Our house isn't big, either: we all have to share bedrooms, so I didn't have my own quiet space to revise in when I was there.

My parents tried hard to keep the house quiet while I revised in the evening and, to his credit, my brother would leave me alone in our room. But my other brother then was just a baby and one of my sisters was a toddler, so there was always some kind of screaming or wailing going on.

I started spending longer at school – I got there as early as I could and left as late as I could – and by doing this I was able to put in enough hours each day. But then there were the weekends. I always took Sundays off (I felt I deserved it), but I liked to try to revise on Saturdays. Unfortunately, school was closed then, and the house seemed to be at its noisiest.

That was when I found the library. My town is pretty small so our library is pretty small too, but it opens from 9am until 4pm on a Saturday, and it felt like the quietest place in the world. Not only that, but there's something about being surrounded by books which I find helps me get in the right frame of mind for revision. They also have an absolutely incredible set of encyclopaedias there, and I referred to them regularly.

I started to get so much revision done in the library that as well as each Saturday I'd also go there in the afternoon straight after school, and then, when it came time for study leave, I went there every day. It wasn't long before the librarians would welcome me by name – I even had a favourite table which they'd try to keep free for me.

I did much better than anyone expected for my GCSEs. In fact, I did so well that I got into a really good college, and when it came time for my AS Levels and A Levels, I knew exactly where I could go to revise.

My brother has just started Year 11. As the second-oldest, he'll start having the same problem as me soon. But the good thing is that he looks up to me, so when I recommend the local library to him as a brilliant revision space, I reckon he'll take my advice.

CHAPTER 16:
THE EXAMS

And so we come to the final stage – your exams. If you're reading this chapter, you've hopefully followed all the advice set out in the previous chapters and are now ready to tackle the exams themselves. It's what you've been working towards for a long time now. And believe me when I tell you that YOU ARE READY, which means that there's not much more left for me to tell you. You've done so much hard work over the past few months, you've put in so much time and effort and energy, and you've revised your socks off. I hope this guide has been useful to you throughout that process. I hope that you've had it beside you in your revision space to check time and time again as you've pushed on with your revision. I hope that it's shown you what you should be doing and when.

Unfortunately, this is where we have to part ways. It's up to you now to do the exams alone. I wish I could write a guide that you could take with you into your exams and regularly refer to and consult just as you've done with this guide during your revision. But we both know that the exam invigilators would never allow that, sadly.

So, before you close this book and put it away (in a safe place – you can definitely use it again for your next set of exams, whenever they may be), I'd like to leave you with some final tips and advice for your exams themselves. Read through the points below, take them to heart, and then put this book down and go on to get those brilliant grades you deserve.

The day before

Reread your notes for the exam you are about to take tomorrow. Now is not the time to try to learn anything new. If you don't know it already, you never will. Instead, look back at what you've already learnt and scan through it. A good idea is to give your notes to your mum and ask her to test you on a few things. Unless you've got more than one exam tomorrow, just focus on the subject at hand.

The night before

Stop revising by 5 p.m. Pack your bag for tomorrow, making sure that you have everything you need for the exam (any books you can take in; any instruments – such as a calculator or protractor – which you are allowed; and at least four pens and pencils, which you've checked are all working). Put all your notes carefully away, pick up your bag and leave your revision space. You will not be returning here again until after the exam. Organise a quiet night for yourself. Ask your parents to make you a hearty dinner. Watch some TV, play a game, have a chat on the phone with some friends. Try not to be in bed any later than 9 p.m. Once you're tucked up in bed, don't be tempted to watch TV, play on your computer or go online. You need a good night's sleep tonight and these will only stimulate your brain and keep you awake. Instead, find something in print you would like to read – perhaps your favourite book, a magazine or even a newspaper. Set your alarm and place it on the other side of the room so that you have to get out of bed to turn it off in the morning. Read for 20 minutes to half an hour. Make sure your phone is turned off so that it doesn't disturb you during the night. Sleep well.

The morning before

Eat a wholesome and substantial breakfast. Try to get the balance right – a single slice of toast is not enough, and a fry-up is too much. A bowl of cereal and some fruit is a wonderful way to start your day and make sure you have the right amount of good energy to tackle your exam. If you're still feeling groggy and not quite fully awake, have a shower. (HINT: A quick blast of cold water at the end of a shower will get your blood pumping around your body, oxygenating your muscles, organs and, most importantly, your brain.) Go to the toilet. If you travel to school with friends, avoid talking about the exam. It's very easy to get worked up and to panic about something when you discuss it with a group of people, so try to talk about anything other than the exam.

REAL-LIFE EXAM TIPS

Give yourself enough time! Always leave more than enough time to get to the exam hall without any rush. You want to be calm when you turn the exam paper over, not in a state of panic.

DAVID

Outside the exam venue

Don't panic. If you've read this far in this book and have followed all of the advice I've given you, then you have done everything you need to. You are ready. If you're still feeling jittery, that's perfectly fine. Sometimes, a healthy dose of nerves keeps us on our toes and makes sure that we aren't going to be complacent. If you've got butterflies in your stomach, then you're in the right frame of mind. You are ready.

At your desk

Once you've found your seat, get your things ready on the desk in front of you. Listen carefully to what the invigilator says – he or she will be giving you good advice about how to approach the exam. Pay attention to how much time you have and look around to see where the clock is. When the exam paper comes to you, read the cover as carefully as you can. If you have time before you are told to begin, read it twice or even three times. Its instructions are incredibly important. Check to see how many questions you need to answer in each section of the exam and read the information again carefully to see if there are any other instructions you need to follow.

The exam

When you are told to begin, open the exam paper and read it through from cover to cover. Pay particular attention to how many marks each question is worth (this should be written as a number next to each question). Quickly work out how long you should spend on each question – for example, in a two-hour exam where the first question is worth 10 marks, the second question is worth 20 marks and the third question is worth 30 marks, you should spend 20 minutes on the first question, 40 minutes on the second question and an hour on the third question. Read each question very carefully.

Remember, you shouldn't just blurt out all your knowledge about that subject, but should answer the question as carefully as possible. (HINT: A good way to do this is to plan your answer before beginning it and then refer to the question during your answer. This will help keep you on track.) When you've done all that, take a deep breath… and begin.

REAL-LIFE EXAM TIPS

Before a practical exam, I used to spend many minutes before in a self-induced, closed-eyes trance, imagining everything going smoothly, anticipating problems and solving them. This put me in a great frame of mind for the exam itself.

STEVE

REAL-LIFE EXAM TIPS

This will probably sound completely obvious, but my biggest piece of advice to any student sitting exams is – STUDY YOUR EXAM TIMETABLE VERY CAREFULLY! I didn't, and I ended up missing one of my exams. Trust me, you don't want to do that. I was lucky that I was allowed to re-sit it at a later date, but I was nearly automatically failed.

SARAH

CONCLUSION: ADVICE FROM TEACHERS

To finish this book, I'm going to mention something that I haven't before. I'm a teacher. I teach English in a secondary school with a sixth form. I told my teaching colleagues that I was writing this revision guide and immediately they began to tell me the things that they would include if they were writing their own. So I'm going to leave you now with some advice from those teachers – people who have devoted their lives to helping students just like you take and pass their exams every single year. I hope you find this advice as useful as you've found this book.

> Don't cram your revision the night before an exam. Take as much time as you can to properly revise each of your subjects.

> Exams are good because they prove to the rest of the world just how amazing my students are.

It's OK not to know what you want to do with the rest of your life. And it's OK if you do know. Either way, treat all your exams as equally important.

My job is to help my students, pure and simple. If they have a problem with anything at all, including their exams, they should come to me and I will help them.

Don't think in terms of right or wrong answers. Think in terms of good or bad answers. Good answers are ones which answer the question set as precisely as possible. Bad answers don't actually answer the question but say something the question never even asked for.

Don't believe what you might read in the papers about exams getting easier. They're not. Exams are just as difficult as they've always been. And our students are heroes for taking them. They should remember that.

Don't ever feel like you're alone when you're facing your exams. Everyone you know has taken exams, is taking exams, or will take exams. Talk to them. Share your experience. You'll realise it's not so bad, after all.

Be confident in yourself. You've been working towards this point your whole life and you know far more than you probably realise.

Exams are important, but not so important that you should make yourself ill thinking about them.

Work hard for your exams, but try to enjoy them, too. This is your chance to really show off just how much you know. And you know a lot.

The students who do the best in their exams are always the ones who have taken it upon themselves to revise the subject outside of my lessons.

And my final piece of advice to you? It's simply this:

APPENDIX: 10 GREAT REVISION APPS

Below is a list of ten great revision apps available for the revising student. They're not only useful, they're also free, and anyone about to sit their exams would do well to have one or two of these on the screen of their phone, tablet or computer. So here they are, in alphabetical order:

Articles
This is basically Wikipedia in an app, although it's much better designed and more user-friendly than the website. It's a very quick and handy way to look up information – although remember what we said earlier: Wikipedia is not always correct.

English Literature Revision Games
This app is of course specific to a single subject, although it can be used by students of all ages. Filled with fun and informative games for a vast range of set texts from GCSE through to A Level, it's a great way to revise whichever book will be coming up in your exam.

Exam Countdown
A great way to keep track of all your exam dates, this app helps keep you focused by providing you with a daily countdown to each of your exams.

GCSE Maths: Revision Questions

OK, so this app is clearly aimed at a specific age group and subject, so it's irrelevant to anyone doing their A Levels. But if you've got your Maths GCSEs coming up, this is an absolutely brilliant resource, and highly recommended.

Gojimo

Covering every major subject from every major exam board, Gojimo contains a vast array of content and quizzes suitable for all students – whether you're about to sit your GCSEs, AS Levels, A Levels, 11 plus or 13 plus Common Entrance. The app's content is even available offline.

iMindMap

Sometimes technology can just help make something like revision less of a chore and a bit more fun. iMindMap is a simple tool – as you've probably guessed, it's a way of creating a mind map on screen rather than paper – but it's beautifully designed and gives the process of mind-mapping a little extra appeal.

Quizlet

While this app allows you to create flashcards for each of your subjects, its real strength is that it also gives you access to the millions of flashcards already created by other Quizlet users.

Remember the Milk

Although this app is for anyone who needs to create a to-do list, many students have found it very helpful for organising their revision. Its key feature is that it can send you reminders via email, text message, IM or Twitter, so it's perfect to ensure you never miss or forget a thing.

Reviser

Reviser is a handy way of condensing your revision notes on to your tablet or phone so that you can revise wherever you are, without needing to take your books and folders with you.

Revision App

It may be the least imaginatively named of all these apps, but it's one of the best. Packed with content made by real teachers, Revision has loads of tutor videos and revision guides for most subjects at GCSE, A Level and 11 plus.

Have you enjoyed this book?
If so, why not write a review on your
favourite website?

If you're interested in finding out more about our books,
find us on Facebook at **Summersdale Publishers** and follow
us on Twitter at **@Summersdale**.

Thanks very much for buying this Summersdale book.

www.summersdale.com